GROWING UP IN A LONDON VILLAGE

PHYLLIS WILLMOTT

Growing Up in a London Village

FAMILY LIFE BETWEEN THE WARS

PETER OWEN · LONDON

ISBN 0 7206 0532 6

PETER OWEN LIMITED
73 Kenway Road London SW5 0RE

First British Commonwealth edition 1979
© Phyllis Willmott 1979

Printed in Great Britain by
Daedalus Press Stoke Ferry King's Lynn Norfolk

CONTENTS

Acknowledgments

Preface   9

1 Forty-Nine   13

2 Sunday   21

3 Out the Front   29

4 Gran   38

5 Out the Back   46

6 Grandad   51

7 Blunham   60

8 Mum   71

9 Outings and Adventures   82

10 Prayers for Pleasures   91

11 Dad   100

12 School   113

13 Looking Back   129

ACKNOWLEDGMENTS

I would like to thank Marie Wain and Sue Chisholm for their willingness and lively interest in typing the manuscript, Peter Willmott for more than I can say, and Beatrice Musgrave, Dan Franklin and their colleagues at Peter Owen for their encouragement and support.

P.M.W.

PREFACE

This book is not, in the narrowest sense, an 'autobiography', but the story of the social world, the time and the place that I grew up in. The social world was that of the largely respectable and mainly skilled working class which began to settle on the edges of London from about the 1880s and which had, by the 1920s, become so well rooted that to the inhabitants of that world it seemed a long-established way of life. The time was the period between the wars. The place was Lee, a district in south-east London.

Travellers in and out of central London, especially those journeying by train, can see a thousand places similar to the setting of this book, for Lee is but one of the apparently endless and (to the stranger) almost identical areas of that older London dating from the Victorian and Edwardian eras which seems to be largely composed of street after street of small terraced houses. A few of these are of red brick but most are built in yellow 'London brick' and virtually all have grey slate roofs and small 'back extensions', also with pitched, slated roofs.

Lee, which covers an area of perhaps a square mile, has increasingly become an amorphous part of the London borough of Lewisham; but until about 1880 it was a village outside London. It once had a 'green' and this corner of the district is still known to older residents as Lee Green. (To newer residents it is more likely to have become 'Lee Gate', the name the local authority has imposed on the new shopping centre it has built there.) From west to east Lee Green is crossed by a main road running from London to the Channel ports of Dover and Folkestone. From north to south, forming a crossroads at

9

Lee Green, runs a road linking Blackheath and Greenwich with outer districts like Catford and Bromley.

Both Blackheath village and Greenwich were in the past larger, more important and more attractive places than Lee ever was. Lee was not much more than a hamlet around the 'green' until the spread of larger Georgian private houses on the Blackheath side first linked it to a more cosmopolitan world. To the west – the London side – the familiar small terraced houses already described had by around 1890 linked Lee to Lewisham and London. But during my childhood the countryside to the east was still within walking distance, although new semi-detached homes, selling at prices from £275, were being built between Lee and Eltham, the next village on the way to Kent.

In later years, as I grew older and moved on to a grammar school outside Lee (and indeed in another borough), my world expanded. But, during the earliest years which are the subject of the book, most of life was solidly based on the small area around Lee Green itself and concentrated within an even smaller triangle of half-a-dozen or so streets bounded by the main London to Dover road on one side, the park of the former manor house on the other, and a street connecting these two on the third.

Despite these boundaries to what we felt to be our local community, the wider district of Lee was, and is still, to a large extent no more than a dormitory area to central London. I am not sure whether it was because we lived in what was the oldest part of Lee that we felt we were still part of a village life, or whether we were influenced by the fact that my grandmother had been raised at Lee Green when it was still a village detached from London. Not only did we know 'everyone' in our own road but most other families in the two or three streets adjoining ours. We also knew by name all the small shopkeepers (the only chain store was Sainsbury's which, at that time, sold butter of different qualities, 'salted' or 'unsalted', standing in large blocks on marble slabs from which the amount asked for was chopped off and patterned into shape with wooden butter patters).

Lee Green had easy access by tram and bus to Lewisham and – a long journey – to London. But Lee Station was an uphill, half-mile walk away and Lewisham Station over one mile. For this reason perhaps, and because many local people were 'old' Lee residents, few of those we knew commuted to London to work but instead, like my father (and his father and maternal grandfather before him), worked locally. It was this combination of factors – old-established residence, living and working within a small area recognized as 'ours', the feeling of knowing and being known by 'everyone' within that area – that created the village-lige setting to our lives.

Apart from a final chapter in which I look back from my present changed position in life, almost everything in this book is based on my own memories of the years between 1924 and 1933, together with the memories and stories passed on to me during the same period – or a few years after – by my mother and other relatives such as my grandmother and grandfather. Young children are receptive listeners and I was no exception. For this reason some of my own most vivid 'memories' are of stories told to me about things that happened to members of my family before I was born. I internalized these 'memories' and so to me they are 'real', but since writing them down I have come to realize, after discussing them with relatives who are still alive, that family stories can vary quite a lot according to who tells them and who listens. This could be something that oral historians have not as yet taken sufficiently into account. To give one example, the story, as I remember it, of my grandfather's career in the army is a mixture of what he told me himself and what filtered through to me via my mother (who no doubt was herself recounting partly what she had heard at first hand from him and partly from Gran, her mother-in-law, or from my father). The story I am left with is that as a soldier of the Coldstream Guards he was at the Battle of Telekebar and that he left the army a sergeant-major. However, when I subsequently sought out the regimental records of his military career a somewhat different story emerged. Although the records were admittedly incomplete, they suggest he could indeed have been at Telekebar but also that as a young man he probably never rose above the rank of lance-corporal and came out as a private, either having been demoted for bad conduct or having himself thrown in his stripe. On the other hand, he did apparently become an acting sergeant when, in middle age, he rejoined the Coldstreams in 1914. In various details, therefore, the reality may not have been exactly the story which I picked up as a child (and which in Chapter 6 is told as I knew it at that time), but despite this the account I have given remains substantially 'true'. True, that is, as far as I can make it on the evidence of my own memories and, equally important, my own perceptions.

Most people seem to feel that their own childhood is in some way special, as indeed it is, since everyone's life is clearly unique. But most do not write about their early years and this raises the question of why I have done so. There are two main reasons, one sociological, the other personal, and the two are interrelated. I was born into what sociologists call a 'traditional working-class family network'. For those born in more comfortable circumstances many kinds of documentary evidence are stored, recording how they lived and what they did. This is not so at all for families of more modest origins. Such families seldom write letters; they do not keep diaries or publish books. My aim in writing *Growing Up in a London Village* is to present some kind of account of that working-class world to which I belonged and, above all, to preserve from oblivion the people who were, for me, irreplaceably part of it.

Forty-Nine

I was far from being 'a love child': my mother once told me that she 'could have knifed' my father at the moment I was in process of being conceived. She was still more angry when she found herself pregnant again so soon after my brother's birth. But by the time I put in an appearance at the nursing home on a hot June day in the 1920s she was on friendlier terms with my father again, and she was hoping for a girl because she knew that he would be pleased. And he was too – tenderly remarking at his first sight of me: 'She looks like a bleeding gyppo.'

'Gyppo', for Dad, meant 'Egyptian'. He spent the last two or three years of the Great War serving with the Royal Engineers somewhere around the Nile. Sick with malaria, he arrived back in England on a stretcher, which he quickly deserted when he heard the announcement over the loudspeaker that stretcher cases were off to an unknown destination in the far North, whereas the batch of walking cases a few yards away were on their way to Ladywell, a mile's walk from his home and birthplace. At Ladywell Infirmary (converted for the war years to a military hospital) his high fever won the battle over the bureaucratic impossibility of his arrival there, and he managed to make his stay stretch for most of the time up to his discharge from the army several months later.

My mother, a tall, anaemic country girl from Bedfordshire with enormous, liquid brown eyes and fine brown hair streaked with gold, was one of the nurses retained from the Infirmary. But the war was over, and she was twenty-six. After some months of shilly-shallying (including fixing a wedding date and then breaking it), Harriet Jane Mann made up her mind to marry Alec Noble, my father. She and Dad found furnished rooms nearby in Lewisham. Nine months later, the landlady below them made it clear she was not having babies in her house, messing up her furniture, and they could get out before, not after, the happy event so obviously imminent. Perforce, the couple accepted Gran's offer of the two rooms and a scullery upstairs in the house where Dad had been born a mile away at Lee. Although it would be nice to have a favourite son home again, Gran was no more pleased at the prospect of sharing her house with her daughter-in-law than the daughter-in-law was. It was to be a temporary arrangement, of course. As it turned out, the temporary arrangement lasted twenty-one years.

Two years and two months after my birth, Mum was back in the maternity home again for her third and last labour. It had been touch and go whether what was owing in fees for her two earlier visits would be paid off in time to ensure a third admission. My mother says that I was taken in to visit my baby brother Joe at the nursing home. I was wearing a mauve shot-taffeta dress Mum had made for me out of a bit of material Dad had knocked off from the dressing room of a London theatre where he had been working. I enchanted the staff not only by my appearance but also by my chatter. Dad, responding to the admiration and praise of his fat-legged, dark-haired little 'gyppo', said anxiously, 'That's the one thing that worries me. She talks all the time – and she'll talk to anyone. I'm just afraid if she'll go off with someone, that's all.'

While Mum was away and Dad was at work, Gran was left to look after Wally (then three and a half) and me in the daytime. By my mother's account Gran's loving care succeeded miraculously and permanently in brushing out all the curls in my hair that Mum had so cherished. My own first memory is of the day Mum returned home from the nursing home with the baby.

Our kitchen-living room at 49, Lampmead Road was a small, narrow room at the back of the house. It, and the even smaller scullery at the end of the kitchen, were part of the 'back extension' commonly added to the red and yellow brick houses which sprang up in their thousands around English towns everywhere from about 1880 onwards. Below us, Gran had an identical kitchen-living room and scullery, except that a small bay window in the kitchen made hers a bit wider, and the lean-to shed outside her scullery door made that much darker. The kitchens tended to darkness because they looked out onto the mirror-image extension of the house next door. But our scullery window looked south, over the long narrow garden. Beyond the fence at the bottom of the garden was the Quaggy, a small tributary of the River Ravensbourne which itself flowed into the Thames.

On sunny days, bright shafts of light splashed through the doorway of the scullery onto our kitchen floor. But the day Mum and the baby came home, although it was August, there was no sun. Or perhaps it was at the end of the day, after work, that Dad went to the nursing home to fetch Mum. Or the scullery door was shut. Wally and I stood side by side, looking across the room. Mum sat in her armchair by the shining black kitchen range, within inches but strangely remote from the two of us clutching hands. On the sombre-covered Edwardian sofa wedged between the wall and the scullery door Dad sat by a white bundle of clothing which looked almost luminous in the dark surroundings. He spoke to us in a persuasive tone – a mixture of gentleness, teasing and wheedling: 'Come on then. Come and look at your little brother.' No words passed between Wally and me; but no words were needed. Wally, I could feel, was resentful. Wally was fixed fast to me or the floor. A baby still when I usurped our mother's lap, he had good grounds for doubting that the new arrival could be to our advantage! It seems ridiculous to think of a two-year-old being aware of ties of loyalty. Yet my memory is strongest, not of the scene itself, but of this sensation of being tugged between the two of them: Wally's tight grip enjoined me to stand fast; Dad's coaxing voice urged me to come. Curiosity tipped the balance. Dad tried again: 'Come on. Aren't you going to come and look at him? Poor little Joey! Look, he's opening his eyes to see you.' I deserted Wally, and ran over.

Three children under four to be washed, fed and kept quiet in two small rooms, with a cold water tap in the scullery above a sink too tiny to hold a washing-up bowl and the only lavatory downstairs along a dark passage and 'out the back'. Mum's day with us was long. Dad left for work early and, in the summer months especially, came back late. After a period of uncertainty and unemployment he had taken up work in the building trade, and at this time was mainly working in large offices and places 'up in London'. We weren't allowed out of bed in the mornings until he had been given his breakfast and left; and we were washed and ready for bed by the time he came home at night. In the mornings Mum did her housework. In the afternoons she took us for walks. Our pram, like our furniture secondhand when it reached us, was blunt-ended and so deep that its belly almost touched the ground. Any number of children, legs hanging over the side here and there, could be – and often were – slung in, plus the shopping as well. After our walk, we came home for tea, played under the table for a while, and then began to get ready for bed. If Dad was home early enough, I could sit by him at the table and watch him eat his dinner. Rather like a pet dog, I could always hope for some kind of titbit if I was not too impatient and worrying. Smoked haddock was a great favourite of Dad's. An enormous, creamy-yellow fish with 'ears' and tail flopping over the edge of the plate was what he liked. He would give me an 'ear' to pick over when he had finished, while he went on to his second course – some kind of salad stuff like cucumber swamped with vinegar, or beetroot or radishes.

Up a half flight of stairs facing the kitchen door were the two upstairs bedrooms. The smaller back room was ours. Gran and Grandad still had the larger front room in which all Gran's children had been born. In our room Mum and Dad slept in a double bed with a feather mattress and, on the corners of the iron bedheads, brass knobs which unscrewed. Joey, at first, slept near the window in his cot but later joined Wally and myself in the single bed pushed against the wall next to Gran's room. We slept two at one end, one at the other. After Dad had seen us, if we showed any reluctance to go to bed when told to, Wee Willie Winkie could be relied on to make us scamper up the stairs. It was quite a time before I realized that the 'knocking at the window' was not Wee Willie himself but my father tapping his fingers under the table. Even when Wally had convinced me that it really was Dad doing it, my excited terror hardly lessened. On more than one occasion when I got to bed, I saw Wee Willie peering in from the window ledge in his black cloak and high, pointed hat. Once or twice I screamed for Mum to come. Amused and tolerant at first, she soon grew tired of this and turned angry, threatening to bring Dad up to see me if there was any more nonsense. Since I feared Dad's anger even more than seeing Wee Willie Winkie there was nothing to be done but to duck under the bed-clothes and lie rigid in terror-stricken silence until sleep defeated fear. Miraculously, it always did.

Saturday evening, when Dad was around to help, was bath night. This was more often than not another time of mixed joy and terror. Before we were any age at all Dad had somewhere found and fixed a large bath in the scullery. It was not an enamelled one or, if it was, it must have been of very ancient vintage, for it was always bumpy and often needed repainting. Soon after the bath came, a further amenity was added by Dad in the form of an ancient geyser. During the week, a wooden top covered the bath and the geyser was almost invisible behind the clutter of bowls, basins and dirty washing in small zinc baths. It was quite a palaver to clear the top and uncover the bath. Once the geyser was lit, and the hot water gushed down, the small scullery rapidly filled with steam and heat. Into this inferno we children were called – one by one. When it was my turn to go in I went screaming. On one occasion I hung in my mother's arms above the steaming water, clutching her desperately and pleading not to go in. She tried persuasion then, suddenly exasperated, gave me a sharp slap. This made me lose my grip on her and she swiftly dropped me into the bath. The spurting blue flames of the geyser, the steam, the hot water, the sting of her slap combined to make me gasp for breath. I still experience a sense of suffocating fear whenever I make the mistake of trying to step into a bath of water a little too hot.

Waiting in the kitchen, my father had the job of drying us one by one as we were handed out to him by Mum. Rosy, shining-clean, and in fresh night-clothes, we were put on the edge of the table to await the next Saturday ritual. According to my mother, both Gran and Granny Mann (her own mother in Bedfordshire) thought her ideas of child-rearing dangerously modern. Mum would not agree, for example, to bandaging her babies' bellies, tightly and continuously, for the first six months of life, as they advised. And she gave her babies orange juice, considered by her elders a highly indigestible ingredient for tiny stomachs. Yet she also carried on with some of the habits sacred to the older genera-tion. Concern over regular bowel movements, for one thing, amounted almost to a fetish. Every Saturday, as we sat on the kitchen table, each of us was handed a little glass of Epsom salts. Every Saturday we protested and argued against taking the bitter draught. Every Saturday Mum and Dad stood there urging us to swallow it all in one big gulp, and held out the sweets we could have to 'take away the taste' as soon as we had done so. Invariably, we shuddered all over at the first sip, and invariably – and at last – we got it down.

We also had to endure in our very early years the ordeal of the brown-paper plaster. Some time in the late autumn large strips of brown paper were cut to a shape to fit our small frames, like a vest or waistcoat. Then, again on a Saturday night after our baths, melted tallow wax was spread on the papers. These 'plasters', while still too warm to be tolerated unprotestingly, were slapped and pressed onto us and left on throughout the winter months to pro-tect our chests from colds and chills. By spring, the brown paper was grubby and worn, and we could begin to pick bits off as the wax broke up. I don't know whether this practice was considered necessary only for the very early years of life, or whether a school doctor, or some such figure of authority, convinced my mother fairly soon that these brown paper plasters were 'old fashioned' and not necessary for warmly-dressed 'modern' children. Whatever it was, by the time I moved schools – I was then eight years old, and Joey just six – brown paper plasters were a thing of the past.

All the terrors of bedtime, and of Saturday nights, had vanished by the morning. Sunday mornings were a time of delight and of lazy, good-humoured calm. We children always woke first on Sunday, and began to push and pummel and giggle together behind the curtain Mum had made, and Dad had fixed to a metal rod which he put up close to the ceiling. After a time Mum, her voice sleepy and gentle, would urge, 'Be quiet you kids. Go to sleep again for ten minutes.' For a while this would keep us in check.

We spoke in whispers to each other, or concentrated our attention on the distempered walls in a search for any oncoming attack from the bugs. Our bedroom was, inexplicably, the only room in the house infested by these pests. In the winter they were no trouble; in the summer they came out in hordes. Upstairs we waged a continuous battle against them. The itching, swelling bites they left on our tender young skins convinced us of their enmity so that, squeamish at first, we soon learned to squash them flat against the wall. If a bug was caught on the way *up* the wall – that is after a recent attack on one of us – bright red blood splashed out under the pressing thumb-nail. As the season continued, the smears of victory (old ones faded brown, new ones still red) disfigured the pale lemon wall and Dad would get out his brushes and start again with the distemper, which was supposed to discourage the bugs as well as conceal the splotches that marked their graves.

Another thing about the bugs was the smell – hard to describe, but fusty and quite unmistakable. It blended pungently with the smell of Dad's bucket of pee under the double bed. On Sundays particularly, the bucket's contents gave out a decidedly beery odour, an inevitable result of his Saturday night's hard drinking 'up the pub'. We quietened down again when a creak from the bed warned us that Dad was climbing out over Mum, and listened respectfully as a new and powerful stream reached the bucket. Then Dad made his way down the half-flight of stairs to get us the great Sunday morning treat – tea for us all, in bed. Curtains were twitched back, laughter, chatter and squabbles mounted as we waited for him to return. The big question was what it would be this week – chocolate biscuits, gigantic round arrowroot, or the pink and yellow 'finger' wafers. We probably got whatever the pub happened to have by the time Dad remembered to buy them, but we always assumed Dad had chosen specially. I liked the arrowroot because they were so big and round and lasted longer, but my favourite was chocolate wafer. How deliciously they crumbled and flaked in the mouth, how perfectly they turned to sogginess with a mouthful of tea. After the biscuits were eaten we could join Mum and Dad in the big bed. Darling, lucky, horrible Joey, because he was Mum's 'baby', went in between her and Dad. He could cuddle up to Mum, even put his fingers into her nightgown and touch her breasts – a thing that would get me a slap and that Wally was too wise to even try. He and I had to be content with the foot of the bed. And with our feet tucked under the eiderdown it was pleasant enough. After ten or twenty minutes of this cosiness (but often interspersed with irritated exhortations to 'stop wiggling'), Mum would get out of bed, go downstairs and soon call us to follow for our breakfast. Dad, left in peace, would once again submerge completely under the bed-clothes and in a flash fall into his habitually deep, half-snoring sleep.

2

Sunday

During the week the centre of our life was upstairs. At weekends, and especially Sundays, downstairs became more important. In the week we saw Gran and the others about the house, most often on our way 'out the front' or to the lav 'out the back'. We could reach the lav either through the side door, and along the outside of Gran's kitchen and scullery, or by using Gran's kitchen and scullery as a short cut. In cold weather – and if we were on good terms with 'downstairs' – we children and Dad always went through Gran's. But Mum, whatever the climate (inside or out) invariably went by the side-way and continually urged us children to do so too.

On Sunday mornings, a comfortable time after breakfast, Gran's kitchen began to fill up with her sons. Her youngest boys (the twins who were born on the twenty-first birthday of her eldest son) were in these early years adolescents and still living at home. Their bedroom was the downstairs room beneath our bedroom and adjoining the 'front room', Gran's cherished parlour. Also living with Gran was her grandchild (our cousin) Peter, two months my junior. Later Peter's brother Kenny came to live with Gran too. The tiny kitchen would already be crowded when we went down. The twins, Dad, cousins Peter and Ken, their father (our uncle Bert) were sure to be there. Sometimes Uncle Len and Uncle Sid (before his job took him out of London) would be there too. All the men were six feet tall but Grandad seemed even bigger for he had weight as well as height. He was almost as proud of his 'corporation' as of his pointed, waxed moustache and imposing military bearing. Once, standing in front of him on a Sunday morning, I touched this 'corporation' with my hand. It was a great surprise to me to find it was soft, like a cushion, not hard and bony as all of my father seemed to be. I poked again with a finger to make sure I had not made a mistake. What was *in* his 'corporation'? I wanted to know. Waves of laughter rocked about the place and teasing suggestions were offered to me – Grandad stuffed his vest with feathers from the chickens he plucked in the shed; it was air put in by the twins' bicycle pump perhaps. When later I asked my mother for her view she cleared up the mystery with a scornful brevity: 'It's *fat* through too much beer!' Amongst her tall and noisy men, Gran would be flitting quietly back and forth between scullery and kitchen, or from the pantry in the passageway into the hall. I never heard her voice raised much above the level of a whisper. She was slightly built and looked even smaller than she was in the midst of her tall sons. Yet above the din of talk and banter she could catch the attention of any one of them the moment she chose to.

The primary purpose of this Sunday morning gathering was alleged to be that of 'saying hello to Mother', but equally important was to decide on the route for our Sunday morning 'constitutional'. The question of which pubs to stop at was each week open to discussion. Were we to get to Blackheath this way (calling first at one of The Tigers – old or new – at the bottom of the hill in Lee, and then at the Hare and Billet on Blackheath) or should we go the other way, calling at the Swan, in Lee High Road, and then the Dacre Arms near Love Lane? We children had no say, but then we didn't expect any. It was enough for us to enjoy the favour of an outing with the men and to know that on the way there would be liberal supplies of biscuits and lemonade and at the end the green spaces of the Heath. Off we all trooped. Dad, as always when scenting beer, was ahead in the advance party, his trousers flapping behind his ankles. The rest of us followed with Grandad, his walking-stick swinging in time to his measured pace, and with us child-

ren and his cocker spaniel obediently at his heel. At the pubs agreed
on for our stops, we children hung about outside, and from time to
time one or the other of the men looked out and handed us biscuits,
nuts and raisins, or lemonade – and disappeared again. Later, I
learned to be ashamed of being a child who had stood outside pubs.
Mum and Dad, in fact, disapproved of parents who spent their
evenings in the pubs with their children left outside, but these Sunday morning 'walks' were regarded as an exception to the general
rule.

When we reached the Heath we raced about with the dog,
chased after each other, and flung stones into the pond at Whitfield's Mount. The dogs – first Beauty and later Prince, her son –
were marvellous to watch. Sticks or balls flung far out in the pond
were retrieved again and again. It was joy to see the intent dark
eyes in the silken head which arrowed out to the floating ears and
again to the wide wake spreading out behind them as the dog
swam back and forth. One Sunday, something went amiss. Uncle
Bert threw out his ebony cane, topped with a heavy silver knob. It
sank. Again and again the dog was sent out, submerged to explore
the muddy bottom and returned, each time more exhausted and
dejected. No luck; the cane was lost. Fifteen years later, the pond
was drained, and the cane returned to Grandad by a keeper who
knew him well and remembered. But by then not only the dog but
Uncle Bert, too, was dead.

Less commonly we would go to the other ponds near Greenwich
Park or the Paragon. In fact we children liked these routes better,
for at one pond we could have half-an-hour on the paddle boats,
and at the other try out the boys' model sailing boats. Whichever
way we had come, whichever paths we took, we eventually reached
our destination – the ex-servicemen's club on the Heath beyond
Whitfield's Mount. While the men drank more beer we children
were pressed on all sides to more lemonade by uncles or old army
friends of Grandad's. As it was a club, we were allowed inside and
sat or stood about staidly and contentedly until it was time to begin
the journey back home. When we were very young, these walks

were no short journeys for our small legs. By the shortest route the Heath was a good mile away and it was an understood condition that we walked there and back without complaints. My own children, used from their earliest years to travelling by car, never acquired the taste for 'nice long walks' with the family that we came so soon in life to regard as a treat. On the way back, the pubs were closed, but we still needed to pass them en route homewards, for both adults and children found it necessary to relieve themselves frequently after so much guzzling. As the only girl, I could be a bit of an embarrassment. The boys were able to dodge in with the men to the pubs' urinals which, being almost always outside, were accessible even when the pubs were closed. Ladies' lavatories were less often so easily available. If necessary, I would be instructed to 'go behind a tree', or 'up the alley', while my brothers 'kept cavey' – and all the time harried me impatiently.

Back home, we would be welcomed by the smell of Sunday dinners. As soon as the front door was opened, the smell of roast potatoes, sizzling meat and boiling greens enveloped us. Upstairs, Mum would be waiting to serve up at once; downstairs, Gran would be almost ready and not so impatient to begin. After dinner, our faces slicked over with a flannel, hair brushed, caps or berets on, Wally and I (and Joey, too, as soon as he was three) went downstairs to get our cousins, and then made our way up the road to Sunday school. The adults, left behind in the unusually quiet house, promptly made for bed. Most of the time I enjoyed Sunday school, although at one period the stories about angelic and intrepid missionaries got me almost as agitated as Wee Willie Winkie had done not long before. I began to dream of throngs of white-draped angels hovering over me. One night (it must have been early, for my parents were not yet in bed) I woke up crying bitterly. 'Wassa matter?' Wally asked me sleepily. 'I dreamt God is calling me to darkest Africa,' I wailed, 'but I don't want to go!' 'Oh shut up,' said Wally irritably.

By the time we had dawdled the few yards back home after Sunday school – and we did dawdle, because on Sunday we

were not supposed to 'play out', which was a real deprivation compared with weekdays – by the time we got home again Mum was
up, bright-eyed and relaxed from her hour in bed, and looking
lovely in fresh, best clothes. Soon we would hear from outside the
call of the winkle-man or the bell of the muffin-man. Wally and I
would dash out to find him, to buy whatever Mum wanted. Outside on a Sunday, in the later afternoon particularly, there was a
quietness that seemed to exude a special, brooding atmosphere.
Even on weekdays traffic was unusual, apart from that of the
roundsmen delivering milk and coal and these were still using
horses and carts, not motor vans, but on Sunday the small streets
were virtually empty.

Before we could have our Sunday tea, Dad had to be roused. If
relations between Mum and him were good, she would go to wake
him herself. More often, as we grew bigger, I would be given the
job instead. I loved it, having learnt from past observation –
supplemented by Mum's detailed instructions as I carefully carried
the cup of tea up the stairs – exactly how this process of 'waking
Dad' must be performed. First, he had to be called; not too noisily,
but with determination. Slowly his nose and then his face would
emerge as he disentangled himself from the sheet. After a suitable
pause, coupled with another call or two, his first mouthful of tea
must be carefully poured into his saucer. 'Dad! Your tea. Sit up.
Come on! Here it is.' The art was to get the first saucerful near
enough to him without spilling any on the sheet, so that he could
sip it barely lifting his head. 'Ahhh!' he exclaimed on swallowing
the first mouthful. 'Ahhh!' when he had swallowed the second.
And so on, until the whole cupful had disappeared, via the saucer,
into the rough-skinned, reddened face, where by this time of day
gilt bristles glinted like splinters all over his chin.

Sunday evening was the high spot of the weekend. Not long
after tea Dad would be off again, with some of his brothers, to 'get
in the beer'. This invariably took longer than promised because if
he or the others met anyone they knew (which they could hardly
fail to do) the code demanded that 'you must have a drink with

them'. Meanwhile in our upstairs kitchen we worried Mum to let us go downstairs as soon as signs of movement and chatter below told us uncles or aunts were turning up. Sooner or later she would give us the answer we wanted, and we trooped down, pushed through Gran's glass-bead curtain which hung across the passage at the bottom of the stairs, and into the front room. It was not a large room, perhaps twelve foot square, plus a shallow bay window area which was entirely filled with Gran's prized aspidistras. There were five or maybe seven in the bay, each set in a large porcelain pot, and for good measure another in a beaten bronze pot embellished the small table set in the centre of the room. This mass of leathery green, whose arching leaves, as far as I could see, never grew but never died, hung about our young heads like palms.

Pictures, family photographs and china plates covered the walls and an ornately carved and mirrored 'overmantel' above the fireplace was crammed on every little shelf with china and brass ornaments – gilt painted jugs, white china swans, coloured glass paperweights, ugly souvenirs from seaside resorts and all kinds of bits and pieces Grandad had picked up during his soldiering years – odd stones or lumps of quartz, 'native' curiosities, exotic shells, regimental plumes. On every scrap of space, on every vertical or horizontal surface in the room, something stood or hung. Even the small space above the door had a picture on it – an unframed oil painting of a cavalier Grandad had 'picked up' from the attic of some grand house he had stayed in during his days as batman to Lord John Somebody. Gran's china was, I now know, fine eighteenth-century stuff which had come to her from her own grandmother. It was treated with the respect its ancestry demanded and never put to use, just dusted and displayed. All in all, the front room was a proud exhibition of Gran and Grandad's pasts, their private museum of treasures.

Their furniture was, of course, like them Victorian. A chaise-longue, horsehair-filled and hard as wood to sit on, with a covering of stiff dark plush that tickled and scratched our young bare thighs. There was one armchair to match the chaise-longue, and half a dozen 'uprights' also with plush-covered seats regimented into any space which could be found to take them. And then, against the wall, the piano with its intricately fretted front, brass candle-racks and ivory keys.

Early in the evening we children were the centre of attraction. We were encouraged to stand by the aspidistra in the middle of the room and sing a song, recite a poem or offer what we could as entertainment. Gran, sitting in her chair beside the fire, was the star spectator; Grandad was the main organizer. More often than not he could not resist taking the limelight from us, bursting into some bawdy song or a rambling and humorous anecdote from his past. By the time all the men had got back from the pub the front room was as awash with people as the overfilled glasses were with beer. Before long someone's voice would rise above the hubbub of laughter and chat and shout out, 'What about a tune then?' Harold, Bert, Sid or Dad would without undue haste move to the piano. Dad was the only one who played from music, but the others – who played by ear – were better, Bert best of all. The musical mixture hardly varied from week to week, beginning with the things Grandad liked most – songs from the old music halls or the war – and moving slowly towards a crescendo of hymns and psalms. The resounding tune of 'Onward Christian Soldiers' was Uncle Bert's special favourite. As his long fingers pummelled the yellow keyboard, his black hair flopped like a bird's broken wing above his brilliant blue eyes. In the damp, white face his mouth became a red cave from which the words poured out. The end of the singing meant, for us children, the end of our time downstairs, although with the continuing clatter of voices and glasses and walking back and forth to the lav 'out the back' it was not easy to do as we were told – 'go to sleep'. Sometimes, very daring, we would creep out of bed and down the stairs, sitting at the bottom to be at least a little closer to the fun. Uncles and aunts, on their way through to the back, would have an affectionate word with us, even give us a biscuit or another drink. But when Gran came through she scolded, and Dad or Mum would soon follow her to round us up to bed again.

Mum, we gradually began to grasp, was not so enamoured of the Sunday evenings in the front room as we were. The money wasted on drink and Gran's queening it over 'my boys' were for her recurrent irritations. Occasionally, and then as time went by more frequently, Mum would refuse to come down until very late in the evening, or even not at all. After a while one of us would always be sent up to get her. It made us miserable to find her sitting alone, her brown eyes soft with hurt, and yet still obstinately refusing to join us. This kind of internecine guerrilla war between Gran and Mum went on all the years we lived in the house. Yet it was not Mum's protests or sulks which put an end to the weekly binges. More powerful forces were needed to defeat Gran's subtle influence and when they came – death and the Depression – they wounded us all more deeply than ever Mum had been. Slowly, as the years went by, the front-room gatherings became rare occasions reserved for birthdays, weddings and funerals.

3

Out the Front

Our front garden, like the one at the back, was long for the size of the house. The straight path from the front door to the gate was bounded on the left by the parallel iron bars separating our path from that of our friend and neighbour, Mrs Jordan. To the right a thick hedge of golden privets and evergreens encircled the garden except under the bay window. The garden was full of ferns growing out of a kind of rockery made from clinkers.

As each of us got to about three years of age we were allowed to begin to 'play outside'. At first, only within the front garden itself, later on the pavement outside, later still up and down the road. Gradually, as our world grew bigger, the path and the front doorstep, and our 'houses' and 'camps' under the thick hedges became places of safety to retreat to when the feuds and hostilities of the street grew too intense or threatening. The path itself was laid with frosted pink tiles each with a white fleur-de-lis in the centre. Sitting on the front doorstep on warm days, simply watching the movements of the busy ants weaving about on the tiles or using a twig to dig out dirt from the grooves in the pattern of the black, iron coalhole lid were pleasant ways to pass less energetic moments. Turning somersaults or other acrobatics on the parallel bars dividing our path from 'Jordan's' was a more active, but still permitted, diversion. Swinging on the gate, using Grandad's trim golden privets as 'armchairs' or setting up 'tents' under the thickest parts of the hedge were frowned upon by the adults. But although these attractive pursuits were forbidden, we often indulged in

them. Experience soon taught us that the risk of being caught in
the act was worth taking, since most of the time the grown-ups
were too involved with their own concerns inside the house to
bother about us outside.

Other children in the road were not allowed to trespass too
freely on our front garden or, for that matter, we on theirs. Next
door, Jordan's two boys and her lodger's two daughters mostly
kept to their side of the bars. Girls were allowed somewhat more
licence than boys; it was usually another girl who kept me company in ant-watching, or some similar peaceful amusement like
making patterns with stones or leaves on the sugar-pink tiles.

Willie Portsmouth's mother, who lived across the road, was far
less fussy about keeping either her front or back garden free of
other children. This lack of fussiness fitted in with her generally
more sloppy ways. She had black, greasy curls, a big flabby body
and sallow skin and was generally believed to be of gypsy background. A gentle, amiable woman with numerous children, she
was not quite up to the standards of respectability of the rest of the
road. She was, it was felt, more the type who should be living in
the 'poorer' road parallel with ours on the other side of the
Quaggy. Far from being thankful to get rid of us into Mrs Portsmouth's sphere, the other mothers, like mine, tried to discourage us
from going over. They preferred us to play on the pavements up
and down the road.

There were about two dozen children of much the same ages in
our road, but not all of them played out as much as we did. Some
mothers, especially those with only one or two children and with a
whole house to themselves, were more fussy and let their children
out only occasionally. But as we all went to one or other of the local
schools, we all knew each other pretty well. One such child with
the to us superior name Leslie, who was not often allowed out but
who walked to school with us every day, caught scarlet fever and
was sent away to an isolation hospital for some weeks. He was a
popular boy and we were all delighted when he returned, but dis-
mayed and mystified at the change in him that had taken place.

No longer friendly, he seemed completely unable to mix with any-one and from then on became a stranger to us all.

In spite of Mum's efforts, my friendship with Willie Portsmouth was intense and long-lasting. He got on well enough with the boys, but he was not so tough as they were and more interested in his pets than in their chief pursuits of fighting, games and collecting cigar-ette cards. The neglected earth-trodden patch of garden at the back of Willie's house could, fortunately for the long-suffering Mrs Portsmouth, be reached by an alleyway which ran along the back of the terrace of houses on their side of the road. Willie had quite a zoo in his garden, and we spent happy hours together cleaning out the rabbit hutches, feeding the chickens, fondling the cats and searching for the tortoise. His love of animals was more than a hobby; it was a passion. He became a junior member of the RSPCA, and then organized me and the others in fund-raising or distributing publicity material. One memorable day a coach-trip was somehow arranged by him (he was then about eleven) to take a party of us to Whipsnade Zoo. The coach arrived outside his house one summer morning and with great excitement we all piled in, Willie ticking us off methodically on his list. We had been sell-ing tickets for weeks before, and to get enough to fill the coach we had to bring in children from the adjoining streets. With many of these we were more often on fighting than friendly terms, and so we set off on the outing with some anxiety. It all turned out very well, and one of the long-term results was a marked improvement in the relationship between the children of 'our' road and the roughs from Hedgley Street.

Organizing 'concerts' was another recurring interest Willie and I enjoyed. One year we formulated an ambitious plan to produce a pantomime. We decided on *Cinderella*. Having, naturally, grabbed the star roles for ourselves – Prince Charming for Willie, Cinderella for me – we next went on to decide who else to include in the cast. My best girl friend, but also something of a rival for Willie's affections, lived just round the corner, in Brightfield Road. Beaty Couldrey had wonderful corn-gold hair. She was also extremely pretty. When I told her on our way back from school of the proposed production she was very interested indeed and not unnaturally assumed herself type-cast for the star role. I hastily disabused her and went on to add that Willie and I had decided she should be one of the ugly sisters. Her face instantly became bright pink, and a second later her hand flew up and clipped me smartly round the face. As she sped off down the road, my rage was now as great as hers, and in a desperate attempt at retribution, I flung my school case after her. It skimmed along the ground, slid under her airborne feet, and tripped her as she came to earth again. Her lovely face scuffed along the pavement and, to my horror, I saw she was badly grazed and bleeding.

By this time we were only a yard or two from my house. Beaty, now in tears, raged against me and sobbed that she was going home to show her mum who would without a doubt be round to see *my* mum. This threat was worrying; it underlined the seriousness of what had happened. Mums could seldom be prevailed upon, in our world, to interfere in quarrels between children. But looking at Beaty's ravaged beauty I feared what Mrs Couldrey's reactions might be on this occasion. I braved it out as best I could, but took the precaution of giving Mum my version of our quarrel as soon as I got upstairs. Not long after, two knocks at the front door took me down the stairs again, very much afraid of who might face me on the doorstep. It was Beaty – Beaty alone, and demanding in her haughtiest manner to see my mother. I had the wit to know that poor Beaty was, in fact, defeated. Clearly, her mother had refused to get involved (or she would have been with her) and I could safely assume my mother would now play a similar hand. Beaty must have known this too, but she did her best to brazen it out and, after some haggling on the doorstep, declared she would not go until she had spoken to my mother. I returned upstairs and Mum, as I guessed she would, said she was not coming down: 'You two must sort it out by yourselves.' Beaty received this message in silence, then turned and flounced away, banging the gate in a final protest. For a week or two we would not speak to each other but then, as Mum would say, we were 'as thick as thieves' again.

The games we played 'out the front' were dictated partly by the time of year and partly by sex, but also by influences and currents that spread amongst us as fast and inexplicably as any virus. Skipping games would for a week, two weeks, a month, be so much our mania that even the boys became infected. Old clothes-lines would be dug out from sheds and cupboards, and the whole width of the roadway taken over by both boys and girls in a ferment of contortionist skills, jumping through or over or in the swirling rope. Most winters someone would appear one day with a 'winter warmer', and then up and down the road mothers would be pestered for cocoa tins and bits of rag. The idea was to punch holes in both ends of the tin, light the rag and keep it smouldering by waving one's arms fiercely back and forth. With luck (and a lot of energetic movement) the tin would give out a little warmth as well as the acrid smell of scorching cloth! Dressing up, hop-scotch, ball games, paper-chases, conkers, marbles: I can't think of any game known to children that didn't at some time arrive – then disappear again – in its season. And according to the needs of the game, and where it began, the little groups about the road would shift up and down, expand and contract, huddle together here or there in a corner, or spread all over the road.

Once a year, in the summer holidays, it would get about that 'the fair' was to begin. The venue for this event was not in our road, but just round the corner into Brightfield. This was because the wall of the end house in our road, occupied by an unreasonably irritable (or so it seemed to us) woman called Mrs French, provided a good background for the side shows. Money changed hands – farthings and halfpennies – for 'a go' in Lucky Dips or raffles, or the chance to buy coconut candy made by some more doting (or less hard-pressed) mum than ours. Girls plied posies of garden flowers, or drinks made from sherbert powder, and both girls and boys made bargain offers of possessions no longer loved. Boys swapped lead soldiers, cigarette cards, marbles made 'special' by their size or markings; girls bargained over dolls' clothes, old prams, pressed ribbons and silver paper to use in their Bibles. The 'fair' usually flourished vigorously for at least a week before slowly dying out. Throughout the boys frenziedly played each other for cigarette cards. The little cards were propped against Mrs French's wall, while the boys, kneeling at the curb, flicked their own cards across the pavement to bring them down. Rare and much desired cards needed to complete collections were played for grimly. Cards which no one valued – 'twicers', or those from sets which, for some reason, no one cared about (wild flowers were often in this category, footballers never) – were squandered by the score in the hope of obtaining a sought-after card. Spirits rose and fell as card-wealth changed hands. As with all those stricken with gambling fever, the millionaire of one day could be the bankrupt of the next.

How Mrs French put up with the noise of the 'fair' outside her house is a mystery. Perhaps she was not as bad-tempered as we supposed. I can see now that what she could not stand, and what brought her out to shoo us away, was playing ball against the wall of the house. Unfortunately for her the expanse of wall provided by the end of her house was an irresistible attraction to us. When the ball season was in swing, it could accommodate three or four girls bouncing balls endlessly and rhythmically against the wall. When Mrs French was in, the reverberation of thumps inside her house must have been unbearable for her, poor thing, but we never realized this. To us she was a stuffy old bird who deprived us of our common rights to use any part of the streets as our own.

In the early years of 'playing out', I had another grudge against Mrs French. She had the wrong name. I cannot explain why but I got it into my head that names ought to fit the things or people they belonged to. I liked it best when I could see this link most clearly, and assumed that it was simply my own stupidity or ignorance when I could see no connection at all. Brightfield Road, I presumed, was so named because it was bright with the sun all day, Lampmead Road because of the gas lamps in it (even though all roads round us had those). Our neighbours, the Easterns, lived to the east of us, I wrongly concluded. But Mrs French was a puzzle because further up our road lived a real French woman – a war bride from the 1914-18 war – who was saddled with another name I have now forgotten. The most tortuous link I remember making was that for Mrs Liversuch. This formidable woman, a near neighbour of my friend Beaty, was so named, I decided, because of the liver-coloured shade of the birthmark on her neck.

It was Mrs Liversuch who tried to frighten me off swigging from the vinegar bottle. The Quaggy (another odd name, incidentally, I never found the clue for) which ran along the bottom of our garden, passed under a bridge over the road where Brightfield ended and less respectable Hedgley Street began. There was a 'corner shop' on each side of the bridge and, like most other residents in the area, we patronized either or both at different times. From the age of three I was sent on errands to 'Mr Burt's' or 'Mr Carter's'. I suppose Dad's daily salad used up a lot of vinegar, and that was the reason I so often seem to remember carrying back a bottle of it along Brightfield Road. Try as I would, I found it almost impossible to resist the temptation to drink some before I got round the corner and into Lampmead, where I would be out of sight of the fearful Mrs Liversuch. More often than not as I stopped to tilt the bottle and satisfy my craving with a greedy gulp, Mrs Liversuch would appear from nowhere. 'I'll tell your mum of you! You naughty girl! You'll dry your blood up, that's what you'll do.' She did tell my mother too, on more than one occasion. Mum agreed that my addiction to the vinegar bottle was not only wrong but unhealthy. As for me, I dreaded the effects on my blood even as I swallowed the stuff. But my will was too weak, the craving too strong. This strange taste eventually subsided, or perhaps it was overwhelmed by my even stronger craving for sweet things.

Mr Carter's shop sold the cheapest sweets. Tiger-nuts, loose sherbet, popcorn or sugar-coated shredded coconut cost a halfpenny for a quarter pound. Even a farthing to spend could offer a choice of liquorice-wood, cheap chocolate shapes or a sherbet dip. When I could afford it I preferred to shop at Mr Burt's. He seldom had anything for the farthing customer, but his choice of sweets was richer. Unlike Mr Carter's, Mr Burt's shop was not built as a shop. He had only the bay windows of the front room of his small house in which to display his wares to passers-by. But inside he had a far greater range of sweets set out on the counter. One winter when money was very short I began to help myself from this counter whenever Mum sent me round on an errand. Once started, it seemed too easy to be true. The trick was to decide firmly what one wanted most from the selection nearest the front of the counter and pick it off quickly when Mr Burt's back was turned. My clever ways came to grief because I did not foresee that Mr Burt must notice the regular depletion of his counter stock. One morning he pretended he had to go into the back room to find something I had come to get for Mum. I was delighted, and greed-ily set about taking advantage of his absence. His hand appeared and trapped mine in the act of removing a chocolate coconut bar. It frightened me out of my criminal ways for good. If he ever caught me again he would come round to see my mother, he said. The thought of my mother's horror, if Mr Burt should have second thoughts and tell her she had a thief for a daughter, was a night-mare which died slowly.

A year or two later we had more trouble with poor Mr Burt. Mum had built up an even larger winter debt with him than usual. One day, sent round for a tin of condensed milk, I came home without the gift stamps she collected and considered her due on any purchase made, even one 'on tick'. She sent me back to ask for the stamps, which I did in the middle of the shop crowded, at this time, with other local women. To my overwhelming shame, in-stead of giving me the stamps, Mr Burt launched into a furious attack on the nerve of customers like my mother who had not paid their bills for months yet still expected to get free stamps. My face crimson, struggling against my tears, I ran out of the shop, over the Quaggy bridge and back home to Mum. She was more upset over *my* experience than her own loss of face. She promised me that, no, she would never make me go to Burt's again. Of course

I did, but it was many months later, and not through any pressure from Mum. Those winter months were hard for all of us in the little roads and houses. Probably Mr Burt was almost as hard-pressed and worried with his debt-ridden customers as they were themselves. I think he regretted his outburst against me in the shop as I fled out of the door. He was certainly always nice to me ever after, which was generous in view of all that he put up with in his dealings with our family.

4

Gran

Gran, my father's mother, was born in Lee. Her mother and father had moved down the hill from Blackheath village after their marriage. Gran's mother's family had owned a saddler's shop in Blackheath village, and Gran's father had been a cabinet-maker. The house at Lee was a cottage on the Blackheath side of the High Street, a few yards from the crossroads and the village green. The green has gone (first usurped by public lavatories and, more recently, by traffic islands), but the phrase remains – the locals still go 'up the Green' to do their shopping. The cottage Gran was born in was – and is – a pretty two-storied terraced building in early Victorian style. Gran, an only child, was spoilt and cosseted in her relatively prosperous surroundings. She never went to school and was barely taught to read or write. Her mother, Margaret Bishop, an unworldly and religious woman, spent most of her time and energies serving the new Congregational Church up in her old village of Blackheath. Gran (christened Ellen but always known as Nellie), was left to her own devices much of the time, with her mother's skivvy to pander to her wants. As a result, in that age of Victorian domesticity, not only did Gran remain virtually illiterate, she never learnt to sew or cook. The only domestic skill with which she embarked on married life was that of being able to dust round delicately with a feather-duster.

As she grew up in Lee, many changes took place around her. Houses were being built at a rapid rate and were soon to surround the village of Lee, engulfing it in 'London's' sprawl. Gran never fully understood what had happened, which was not so surprising since she spent her entire life within a mile, at most, of Lee and Blackheath. She seldom went as far as Lewisham, which to her was the next place on the way to distant London, and probably the furthest journey from home she made was when my mother once took her, for some ailment, to the outpatients' department of the Miller Hospital in Greenwich.

One building familiar to Nellie from her childhood was the police station. It stood almost opposite her home on the other side of the High Road. To this station came a new recruit, an ex-sergeant-major, recently retired from the Second Battalion, Coldstream Guards. I don't know how Walter Noble, my grandfather, met Nellie but living opposite each other they could hardly have failed to get acquainted. However it happened, Grandad rapidly charmed his way into the favour of the cabinet-maker Sidney Bishop and his religious wife Margaret, married Nellie, and later rented and moved in to one of the new terraced houses built in Lampmead Road in 1889. A year after the marriage, the first baby, a girl, was born and died. Then followed Sidney, Walter, Jack, Len, Alec (my father), Bert and the twins, Harold and Bern. My father remembered visiting the saintly Granny Bishop in her cottage in Lee High Road when he was still small enough to play under the furniture, and where he once found – and was allowed to keep, so he said – a gold half-sovereign that had been lost in a corner. When her husband died, Margaret Bishop moved into her daughter's house. Margaret Bishop grew increasingly fond of her son-in-law Walter, and was blind to faults in him which, had she recognized them, she could not possibly have condoned. The fact was that, more than most men of his time, he needed a greater stimulus in conversation and in company than Gran could provide, and he found what he needed in the local pubs. A favourite anecdote of his was of the night he came home so drunk that, having opened the front door, he fell down in the passage and couldn't get up again. Hearing the noise, his mother-in-law came out from her back bedroom downstairs and asked: 'Walter, my dear boy, whatever is the matter?' To which he replied, 'Mother, I don't know. I think I must be paralysed.'

Margaret Bishop died with her affection for her son-in-law undiminished. He, for his part, never failed in recollecting her to remark 'She was an angel!' She left her money – a bag of sovereigns – to him. They did not last him long but, ever a sentimental man, he had a hole drilled through the last half-sovereign and wore it on his watch chain.

How helpless, ignorant, tiny little Nellie managed through the early years of her married life it is impossible to understand. Even when we had arrived on the scene, and her family obligations were much lighter, she spent all day on Monday getting through her washing. This, and her consistent capacity for burning something at almost every meal she cooked, were continual stimulants to my mother's scorn. As sure as the smells crept up the stairs, her same phrase would come too: 'Gran's (or if Dad was present, 'Your mother's') burning things up again.'

One of Gran's grievances against life, borne like the others with a quiet air of martyrdom, was that her only daughter had died so soon after her birth. She always managed to imply that whereas her sons had all deserted her, had her daughter lived she would have been around to care for Gran in her old age. Mum was, in practice, very good. She nursed, or at least advised, the whole household in times of illness. She took Gran or our cousins Pete and Ken to the hospital whenever this was necessary, as well as us 'upstairs'. But, of course, these were duties which Gran felt her own daughter would have carried out not merely with good grace but with love. In the front-room gatherings on Sunday evenings, after her third or fourth 'tiny drop' of whisky had vanished, Gran was particularly prone to mourn her loss. Sometimes, when exacerbated beyond her limit, Mum would snap out, 'If your daughter had lived, she'd be married like the rest of us. And probably too busy with her own kids to worry about you.' Gran would look at her reproachfully, purse her lips in silence, and turn her head away.

Gran's professed longing for a daughter was not to be compensated by me, her nearest granddaughter. I suppose I was too tainted with my mother's influence; or possibly with my brown eyes I bore too close a physical resemblance to my mother to be an acceptable substitute for her own lost girl. That the relationship between Gran and I was always uneasy was certainly partly because I could not help but see Gran through my mother's eyes.

One of the things Mum couldn't stand was Gran's absolute quietness. It was unbelievable how silently she moved about the house. We could open our kitchen door and find her there without having heard a sound. Mum was convinced that she listened outside our door and even 'poked around' in our rooms when we were out. But downstairs she was much the same. She moved about there too with the same swift utterly silent movements. Again and again, rushing noisily 'out the back', I would unexpectedly come face to face with her in the darkness of the passage. We would each draw our breath in sharply, both of us always a little startled. More than once I nearly knocked her flying down the three steps by the cellar door. Flitting quietly in and out, she could catch you by surprise coming out of her bedroom, or her front room, or up from the cellar where she had been to get her butter or to put a shilling in the meter. Even when we were 'out the front' we could not escape these unexpected encounters with her. Dusting round the front room, peeking out on us from behind the curtains, she would suddenly 'appear', tapping fiercely at the window, to stop us doing whatever it was she had caught us at – lifting the coalhole cover, sitting in the hedge, trying to unwind the young uncoiled springs of the ferns.

One day, when I was hanging about in the passage, unable to make up my mind whether to go 'out the front' or 'out the back', Gran appeared at her bedroom door. She pursed her lips into a smile and greeted me in her most friendly terms. 'Hello dear, what are you doing?' 'Nothing,' I answered, immediately and unreasonably feeling vaguely guilty. She indicated silently to me to stay where I was, and retreated into the darkness of her room where I could hear her rummaging in a drawer. When she came out again, she had a tissue paper packet in her hand and moving off to her kitchen signalled me to follow. She sat down in her chair by the table and began to unravel the paper in her lap.

I waited expectantly, and began to hope that some precious piece of jewellery was going to emerge, perhaps even to be given to me as a special mark of the affection I wished she had for me. I knew Gran had some pretty pieces, mostly Victorian brooches, her mother had left her. Mum had always hinted that many more I had not seen were hoarded away in Gran's drawers. Suddenly, out of the paper, hair spilled over Gran's old and freckled hands, over her drab old skirt. Long, human hair, bright, live, and auburn-red; young and straight and shining. My first feeling was, of course, of disappointment, but this was rapidly erased by a puzzled curiosity. 'Whose is that?' I asked. To my utter disbelief Gran answered proudly, 'Mine.' This struck me dumb. Gran's hair was white, or more accurately, a yellow-grey, and had always been so as far as I was concerned. I looked again at the switch of auburn in Gran's lap, looked again at her head of thin, grey hair scraped back into a tiny bun on the scrawny neck. For the first time I struggled with the fact that Gran had, incredibly, once been young.

Very young, it turned out, when the auburn hair had been cut off. She told me how she had had it cut off when she was seventeen, and her grey eyes sparkled as she recalled her mother's shock and anger at this outrage. She never did explain why, some half a century before the fashion for short hair began, she had performed this violent act. And I have never been able to decide whether the expression of quiet relish, perhaps even malice on her face, was for the memory of that one openly rebellious moment in her life, or the satisfaction at my own incredulous astonishment.

In Mum's eyes Gran was a 'crafty bitch'; to Dad and his brothers she was feminine fragility personified; to me she was an enigma. To my cousins, Pete and Ken, she was the only 'mother' they really knew. When my mother and father met at Ladywell, they were to set in motion an unusually close union of families. Not long after Mum and Dad married, my mother's older sister,

Bertha, met and married my father's eldest brother Sidney. And a little later still, my mother's youngest sister, Pam, married Dad's younger brother Bert. Granny Mann, Mum's mother, asked when the third marriage between the three brothers and the three sisters was arranged, 'Are there no other men in London than these Nobles?' Pete and Ken were the children of the youngest pair, Bert and Pam, and (like Bertha and Sidney's children, Peg and John and Dorry) were our 'double cousins'. From the beginning Bert and Pam's marriage ran into difficulties. They were always quarrelling and running away from each other. I remember one morning we woke up to find Auntie Pam in bed with Mum and Dad – with Mum, of course, in the middle.

Both Pam and Bert were attractive, intelligent and 'highly strung'. The attraction between them was intense yet they seemed unable to live together happily. Their first child, Peter, was born some weeks prematurely and for this reason was given into Gran's experienced hands to rear through his precarious early months. He was so small, it was always said, that he could be put into a quart-sized jug. It seemed to me an odd way of measuring a baby, and although I never asked I half imagined they had found out by using such a jug to bath my tiny cousin in! He survived, so Gran must have learnt something from her long years of childbearing if little else. Later, when things were going well between his parents, Peter went to stay with them in their flat nearby, but his home remained with Gran. Some two years later Ken was born. His first two years of life were spent with his mother, but from then on he was shuttled back and forth between her home, Granny Mann's and Gran's. When he was five, his father, Uncle Bert, came back to live with Gran after another row. Auntie Pam, overcome with despair, left Ken to have tea with us, borrowed sixpence from my mother and went home alone to gas herself.

For the next two years the little house was crammed full with its complex of relatives. In our upstairs bedroom slept Dad and Mum and we three children. In the 'big' front bedroom, Gran and Grandad found room for Pete and Ken. The downstairs bedroom which had earlier been that of Gran's mother, Margaret Bishop, the teenage twins now shared with Bert. Gran's family, which had seemed to be diminishing, had once again grown large. Once again she was the centre of a masculine world.

Gran never forgave Pam for her suicide, but to my mother it was a dreadful blow for which she sometimes unfairly blamed herself and at other times, and equally unfairly, Gran's interference. This interference consisted chiefly in the fact that Gran had welcomed Bert back to her home whenever he and Pam decided to part again. No more, in fact, than Mum herself had done for her sister on the night she flew to her. Even Gran's taking over the care of Peter was suspect when Mum's mood was black against her mother-in-law. Dad, like all of us (apart from Gran), was fond of his vivacious and wild-spirited sister-in-law, but he too felt that the shameful blow she had struck at our family by her suicide was unforgivable. After what I now realize was the day of the funeral (when, for once, we were surrounded in our upstairs kitchen by Mum's relatives), no one spoke of Pam. She seemed, to us children, to have been there one day and then to have vanished for ever. It was only gradually that we realized she was dead.

Gran, being over sixty at this time, naturally had her own ideas about how her little grandsons should be reared. She was decidedly fussy about hair being brushed shining-flat, shoes being highly polished, legs being well covered with long woollen socks, and 'plenty of warm clothing' winter and summer. Here was yet another source of tension between Mum and Gran. Peter and Ken, being her sister's children, were also of close concern to Mum. Indeed, Gran depended on Mum to carry out responsibilities for the two boys. School medicals, visits to hospital, clinic or the doctor were always put on Mum. And during holidays when she took us out for picnics, shopping or sightseeing expeditions, she seldom had the heart to leave Pete and Ken behind and so usually she went off with all five of us. But *in* the house, the boys lived 'downstairs' and we lived 'upstairs'. When we played inside on rainy days, we used the common parts of the house – the stairs and passages, the landing by the upstairs bedrooms, and occasionally the cellar. It was only on birthdays we ate together – upstairs or downstairs, according to whose anniversary it was. Mum's teas were generous spreads of tinned fruit, jellies, home-made cakes and trifles. Gran's constant 'treat' for birthday teas was bananas sliced up in a dish of cream. As usual Mum's contempt for Gran's limited culinary imagination was profound. I never dared to confess that Gran's simple dish of bananas and cream I, for one, found as invariably delicious as Gran herself obviously believed it to be.

Mum always implied that Gran's great feat was the way in which she managed throughout her life to pull the wool over her sons' eyes. Certainly, these six-foot-tall, heavy-drinking, hard-working men treated Gran with an unbroken protective gentleness and deference which their own wives were never granted. This would have been tolerable, in Mum's view, had Gran really been the gentle little lady she pretended. The paragon who never raised her voice, did not drink or smoke, and sat quietly in a corner while her menfolk bragged and argued round her was, according to my mother, nothing but a hypocrite. The paragon who 'didn't drink' imbibed on Sunday nights enough in her 'tiny drops' of whisky to make any of her daughters-in-law drunk. The paragon who never raised her voice could be heard daily and monotonously scolding Grandad in the kitchen. Mum even went so far as to maintain that she was a 'secret drinker' whom she had caught on more than one occasion 'up the Green' popping into The Tiger for a solitary nip. There can be no doubt that Gran did go off 'shopping' and disappear for hours. Mum, on her more charitable days, believed she wandered up the hill to Blackheath village to visit friends of her childhood unknown to us. In so many ways she was a secret kind of person; a bird encaged by her own odd upbringing. I can see her now, sitting in her chair, one of her mother's delicately crocheted shawls round her shoulders, pretending to read the newspaper or, genially encouraged by Grandad, nervously and painstakingly 'signing' her name on a document. And I can feel again her repressed rage as we stood and watched her.

5

Out the Back

'Out the front' was our domain – the children's. The front room was Gran's. 'Out the back' was decidedly Grandad's. Probably, if I went back there today, the garden would seem tiny. Then, it seemed huge. Or at least large enough to be divided in my mind into five distinct parts.

First of all came the narrow bit running from 'our' back door alongside Gran's kitchen and scullery. Just outside, facing the door, was our coal bunker, large and strong and built by Dad out of discarded railway sleepers (Gran's coal was shot straight down the hole outside the front door and into the cellar). Dad's bunker held a ton of coal. Not that we could afford that amount in one go. Mum filled it up several hundredweights at a time during the summer months. When we ran out in the winter more often than not we would have to borrow – or pinch – a bucketful at a time from Gran's supply in the cellar. Alongside the path by Gran's kitchen was a narrow strip of sunless earth. Virginia creeper covered the high fence dividing us from our neighbours, the Easterns, and in this patch of earth, bluebells – or, more exactly, bluebell foliage – flourished abundantly. Nothing else did. This useless strip of ground Grandad gave to us children to use as we chose. All our attempts to grow seeds or plants (other than bluebell leaves) failed completely. But it was not a bad place for digging holes to reach Australia, or for making mud pies. Each autumn the Virginia creeper transformed the fence into an exotic blaze of red, and it was nice then to think that this was 'ours'.

The doorless shed outside Gran's scullery was the second part of the garden. It had a corrugated iron roof, and it was full of a clutter of Grandad's garden tools, Dad's shoe-mending tackle, an enormous round knife-grinder and cleaner, Gran's zinc baths and the mangle. In one corner of the shed, itself enclosed and turned into a sort of dark cupboard by the shed surrounding it, was the lavatory. It was dark for there was no window to start with and the shed cut down even more what daylight could penetrate the gap above the door. We all left the door ajar unless we heard the sound of anyone else approaching. While undisturbed, it was just possible with the door open to read whatever items of interest turned up on the pieces of newspapers neatly cut and stacked in a wooden box – another of Dad's improvements – on the left-hand wall. On the right-hand side there was a sort of pink-tinted cartoon in a proper wooden frame. I never succeeded, because of the dim light, in making out what it was about. It was inconvenient having only one lavatory. Adults expressed their anger with us children with great force. Either one of us was always 'in there' when they wanted to go, or one of us would interrupt them with urgent demands to 'be quick' when they had hoped for a leisurely and enjoyable session in peace. Grandad in particular was enraged when disturbed: 'Bloody kids,' he would bellow for the whole road to hear. 'Can't even have a good shit in peace in this house!'

Outside the shed, the third part of the garden provided the community area for the use of children and adults alike. It was a square of ground about twelve feet by twelve with a hard surface of packed ash and cinders in the centre. Privacy from our neighbours was secured by more of Grandad's beloved golden privets; this time growing to a height of four or five feet, and with a flat top a yard wide. In the corner by the shed there was a gap in the fence. A wooden step ladder set against our side of the fence gave access to 'Jordan', Mum's friend as well as our neighbour. Jordan had a side entrance to her house and, within strictly understood limits, we could use her side-way to get into our house if necessary. We children sometimes abused this privilege when coming back home. If in the excitement of playing out, one had ignored a call of nature dangerously long, it was tempting to run down Jordan's side-way and pop over the fence to the lav. The alternative was to be hopping up and down on the doorstep, literally holding oneself, while someone inside took their time in coming to open the front door. All the same, if this short cut was used too often, Jordan would mention it to Mum who would tell us off and make us go back to using our own front door again.

Alongside the step ladder was Beauty's kennel. When we were very small we sometimes crawled inside and used the kennel as 'our house'. It had a strong dusty and doggy smell inside, which I liked. But Mum and Grandad turned us out as soon as they found us there. Grandad considered it unfair to deprive his dog of her hideout; Mum was afraid of us picking up worms or fleas, and also rightly believed that the inside of the kennel was 'filthy'. Sometimes rats found their way up from the Quaggy and, attracted by the food scraps round it, settled in under Beauty's kennel. Whenever Grandad realized rats were nesting there again the men gathered on the cinder patch and, under Grandad's command, dug down to the rats' nests. Helped by the dog they enjoyed themselves killing the rats as they came out. During the ratting women and children were shut up indoors, but the tension and excitement out the back was transmitted into the house and was frightening.

On the south-eastern and south-western corners of the cinder patch two bushy lilac trees lorded it over the golden privets. Under each tree, indeed embedded in them, were green benches built by Dad out of the seat backs of rowing boats – probably got through Grandad's connections with local park-keepers. The benches were primitive structures, leaning slightly inwards against the lilacs, narrow-seated because of their original use, and curved on all edges. A small gate, flanked by the golden privets, opened onto the fourth part of the garden. This part was specially Grandad's. The narrow cinder path down the centre was edged on either side by the flower-beds, which were his pride and joy. Enormous clumps of peonies, canterbury bells, antirrhinum, phlox, gladioli, sweet-william, brown and yellow helenium, marguerites, gypsophila, pinks and carnations flowered in summer and enchanted our eyes on the occasions we were allowed to follow Grandad and other admiring adults in staid procession down the path beyond the little gate.

The garden narrowed towards the end and, where the fence concealed the banks to the Quaggy, the garden was only about six foot wide. These last few yards were the 'kitchen garden', where Grandad grew jerusalem artichokes, runner beans and marrows, and where rhubarb, mint and loganberries flourished almost unaided. When I was big enough no longer to be a threat to Grandad's flower-beds, Mum would send me down to pick the mint for new potatoes or mint-sauce, or to pinch a few loganberries. When we were small and still under escort, Grandad himself would scratch our names with a matchstick on the small marrows so that we could watch them grow larger as the marrows did.

Before we had grown big enough to prefer the wider world, the greater freedom of 'out the front', the boys and I found adventures and fascination 'out the back'. It was here that the thick privets first tempted us. We crept beneath them, sat in the golden gloom and chatted and quarreled and played. 'Mothers and fathers', 'doctors', 'naughty boys' were recurring favourites. As the only girl I was always 'mother'. They seemed to like strong discipline, and to enjoy having their bums smacked! Playing 'doctors' we could reverse roles a bit more. The boys could play 'doctor' and examine my crotch, or I could be 'nurse' and return the compliment by looking at their penises. As far as I can remember no one ever caught us playing these dubious games, but we knew instinctively that they were not the kind adults would smile upon. Which is why we chose 'secret' places for them, like under the bushes or (on wet days) inside the cupboard on the upstairs landing, a place crammed with old army coats and suitcases full of picture postcards belonging to Gran and mostly sent to her by her sons during the Great War.

Out on the cinder patch we had plenty of other amusements.

One favourite was to find snails from the lilac trees and have races with them along the seats of the wooden benches. Sometimes we cracked their shells on a stone and then peeled off the pieces for the fun of it. Grandad, if he saw us, had no sympathy for the snails – which were 'pests' – but he did object strongly to the silvery tracks of slime our snail-races left on the seats. 'Dirty little buggers! Clean up those seats or I'll tan your hides till you can't sit on them,' he would shout over our heads.

6

Grandad

Grandad's violent language and loud voice were belied by his actual behaviour. I do not know whether he had been, in the past, a severe father to his sons. But to us, his grandchildren, despite his bellicose ways, he was invariably soft-hearted and affectionate. Gran, with her quiet voice, could lash us with her sharpness and we were always a little afraid of her. Grandad, shout and swear as he would, never frightened us at all. It's true that when he was most noisily angry at some offence of ours we would try to put things right, but this was out of our affection for him rather than from any fear.

Grandad, unlike Gran, was not a native of Lee. He was born in Suffolk near to the Norfolk border-town of Diss. He came from a prolific line of poor and illiterate people who had lived out their lives within the village and others nearby for over 250 years. If they were men, they worked on the land as agricultural labourers, if women, as servants until they married and moved on to their own private treadmill of childbearing and domestic toil. Grandad's father was one of this long line of agricultural labourers who, not untypically, died young. At the time of his death, aged thirty, from tuberculosis, Grandad was not yet two years old and the youngest of seven children. An eighth child was born a few months after his father died. Some five years later Grandad's mother remarried and began to produce more children. Grandad's stepfather had little time for his unruly band of stepchildren and drove them away to work as soon as he could. Grandad, on his side, hated this man and grew up regarding his grandfather, William Noble, as his only real father.

Unlike the rest of the family, William Noble had done well. He too began his working life as an agricultural labourer but by his mid-thirties he had secured a job as farm bailiff, and later became the steward.

Grandad's imagination was vivid, and my mother for one always urged us to take anything he told us with a pinch of salt. True or imaginary, he often told us that when he was a child the squire for whom his 'father' worked would ride through the village cracking his whip to clear his way of children or any other obstacles, such as cats or dogs, who crossed his path. Sent away to work at eleven years old, Grandad found it hard to settle when he came back. By the time he was sixteen Grandad had apparently had enough of squire and stepfather and he 'joined the colours'. At this time of his life he was illiterate, but once he reached London he felt the need to be able to read and write. He said that he taught himself to read by studying hoardings and posters as he walked about, but perhaps the army itself added a few lessons. However it was, he became an avid and incessant reader, a good letter-writer, and an outstanding raconteur and conversationalist. One of his proudest boasts was that he not only could, but had, 'conversed with the highest in the land'.

The unit Grandad joined, and of which he was inordinately proud, the Second Battalion, Coldstream Guards, had a motto which we soon learned meant 'Second to none'. By the time he left the regiment he was a sergeant-major but still a young man. He talked often of his exploits and of the campaigns and battles he had been active in. Again, Mum said he made most of it up, or got the ideas from the historical novels he was always reading. Perhaps he embellished his experiences, perhaps he simply related what as an imaginative man he had 'seen'. But there was no denying his hoard of medals, or his old trophies decorating the front room, or his red feather plumes from the regimental 'busbys'. A phrase often used by him sooner or later in any of his army anecdotes, and which

remains to haunt me, was 'that night we lay at Dover'. As a child
this little comment never failed to bring to my mind a vivid picture
of the footsore soldiers unrolling their blankets onto the hard
ground to 'lay for the night' on whatever spot they found themselves.

Grandad must have made an impressive figure in his uniform.
About six foot tall, his bearskin adding another foot at least, and
with his perfect upright bearing, he must surely, as he claimed,
have unnerved many a young recruit. There was a framed photograph in Gran's kitchen of a slight, straight, fair young man in a
tight military tunic, drainpipe trousers and a pillbox hat. This, I
was told (but found difficult to believe), was Grandad as a young
man. It's true that, like Grandad, the young man had a moustache,
but even this was but a shadow of the fine twisted and waxed affair
that adorned the upper lip of the Grandad we knew. The photograph must have been taken when he was still in his teens.

The high-spot of Grandad's 'active service' in the army was un-
doubtedly the Battle of Telekebar when, according to his typical
fullbodied language, 'the river ran red with blood', and 'pipettes'
were issued to the men to purify water for drinking. At this time
he would have been barely twenty years old. The high-spots of
more peaceful periods of service were those when he 'lay' at
Wellington Barracks with all the pleasures and vices of London to
enjoy.

The experiences of travelling about the world and of meeting
all kinds of men – and all classes of men – changed Grandad, in his
view, from a country bumpkin into a man of the world. There was
in fact much of the countryman about him throughout his life
(many of his favourite phrases were pure Suffolk) but he did learn
a lot more from his army life than just how to read and write.
Probably the most important influence on his own way of life was
that of meeting at close quarters officers of the Guards who were
indisputably gentlemen too. Grandad's close observation of the
way of life of the upper class made it clear to him that two things
separated gentlemen from the rest. First, they went to something

called 'varsity' and secondly, they took their leisure as seriously as some less-endowed men took their work. As a result of this knowledge, Grandad, unlike most men of his class, far from fearing retirement aimed at reaching it as quickly as he could. For some years after leaving the Guards he was a police constable at Lee. He resigned from the force on being instructed one night to 'bring in' some poachers with whom he was on most amicable terms in the Grove Park area of his beat. A little later he took to another uniform – this time that of park-keeper at Ladywell Recreation Ground. At the outbreak of World War I he offered his services to his country once more and, no longer young enough for active service, obtained an enviable position as quartermaster sergeant.

The war was not so gentle to some of his sons. Bert's lungs were weakened by the rigours of the Russian winter which subsequently led (although this was never proved to the satisfaction of the administrators of war pensions) to the tuberculosis which orphaned Pete and Ken. Dad's malaria, picked up in Egypt, attacked him periodically for years after his small disability pension was declared by the same war pension judges to be no longer justified. Affecting Grandad more closely, two unmarried sons were killed. John, the second son, a brilliant boy who had gone with a scholarship to the nearby public school of St Dunstan's College, and who reached the rank of captain in the army, died at Ypres. Another son, Watty, was also killed.

Saddened though he was at his losses, Grandad found he had thereby gained two more small pensions to add to those he had collected on his own behalf. Though still in his fifties he decided his working days were done. Some guile was required to ensure that all the pensions rightly due to him, in his view, were paid. Then, as now, officials in charge of pension funds had an unlikeable tendency to stop any pension they could prove to be unneeded. But they were probably less efficient then, for certainly Grandad succeeded in drawing not one or two but several pensions for the quarter century and more of his long retirement. With this steady income, the fruits of services rendered to his country by him and his sons, Grandad became, in his mid-fifties, the 'gentleman of leisure' he had learned to admire in his army days.

Leisured, but certainly not lazy. The habits of his early life were too ingrained for that. He got up at six each morning, Sunday not excepted, and made a cup of tea for 'Nellie'. From then on, according to the time and season, his orderly pattern for the day went into motion. A good many household chores, the heavy cleaning, polishing of shoes and boots, turning the mangle on Monday washday, were some of the jobs Grandad did to help the dreamily feeble Nellie. Then there was the work in his garden, the regular 'constitutionals' to exercise man and dog, the fetching and carrying of 'empties' and refills of the daily Guinness required for lunch. Also the social demands of the 'local', the daily perusal of the newspaper to keep abreast of 'public affairs', and the endless pleasure of books and more books.

In summer, any fine morning at about eleven, Grandad could be found sitting on the bench under the lilac ('lilock' he called it) reading the morning paper. Legs apart, the better to balance the weight of his 'corporation', baggy flannels tightly belted over it, in a clean, black-striped shirt (without a collar but with a collarstud at the neck) he would sit there reading until the position of the sun told him it was time to move on. Then he would go inside, put on his starched white collar, brush his hair, his jacket, his stiff trilby hat with the rolled brim, buff up his highly polished shoes, give his moustache a final twirl, put on his jacket and hat, pick up his ash stick, pull himself fully erect, call his dog, and go out up the road to the off-licence. The contrast was striking between the slackish apple-faced 'private' man who shuffled about the house in slippers and worked in the garden and looked like any country yokel and the erect, dignified figure who faced the outside world, unimpeachable in dress and manners, the man of substance respected by all who knew him.

Always after lunch a peaceful lull would emanate from downstairs. Gran and Grandad were taking their afternoon nap. But by three o'clock Grandad would, if the weather was fine, be outside in the garden again. Working in the garden, if work was to be done, or sitting on the second bench on the west side (now in the shade of the other lilac bush) reading his book.

With the same regularity that distinguished all his behaviour, Grandad worked at the massive task of keeping his hedges of golden privet and variegated laurels trim and neat. During the summer he cut those 'out the back' one week, and those 'out the front' the next. This was a job he usually carried out in the late afternoon when the heat of the sun had gone. He would come out, sleeves rolled up to his elbows, a battered panama on his head if the sun still shone, carrying brushes and shears, and then an armful of zinc baths and buckets from the shed. His constant care of them had made our privets a solid mass of yellow, which the sun on hot days turned to shields of dazzling brass. As he trimmed away, he would give them a shake every few minutes to make the cuttings fall through to the ground. If he found any suspicious dents where we children had been lounging back in bushy 'armchairs', he would mutter loud and rudely about the ways of the 'bloody kids' he was forced to endure. He would at the same time be pulling and pummelling at the dent to get it back into line with the elegant curves of the rest. In time, we learned how to do this remodelling ourselves and could therefore cover up the worst effects of our sitting in the privets. At the end of the shearing, the privets were once again barbered to perfection. Grandad had such an eye that the curves and lines were flawless from the rounded tops to where, still dense and abundant, the gold leaves touched the ground. Sweeping the debris of leaves into piles, then shovelling them into the containers was a job we were sometimes privileged to help with, but Grandad really preferred to do it alone. It was too often a temptation to us to forget the main purpose of 'clearing up' and wallow in the baths full of golden leaves, or to begin a 'battle of leaves' by throwing handfuls at each other. Although impatient with us, and anxious to get on, Grandad sometimes got caught up in savouring our enjoyment. Wrathfully bellowing at us though he might be, he was struggling too to suppress from his watering blue eyes the enjoyment of our joy.

One of the nicest things about him was that his humour always extended to jokes against himself. If, as he came bellowing out at us, he tripped over a bucket of trimmings he himself had put ready to take next, his language and rage would reach the heavens. Later such incidents became prized anecdotes for uncountable re-tellings. Grandad's helpless amusement would then invariably increase the general hilarity these accounts produced, far beyond any intrinsic humour the incidents themselves in fact possessed. Grandad's great frame, and particularly its fatty parts – his belly and round freckled jowls – would shake with his laughter, his watering eyes would flood over and he would fumble in pockets to find his spotted handkerchief to mop at his eyes, his face, his sandy but balding head. One story of disastrous fun would lead to another: 'What about when the jumping-jack chased you round the bonfire that Guy Fawkes night, and you nearly fell in?' 'And remember when Wal's "ghost" in the cellar made you trip up the stairs?' Even Gran, as we all stood or sat, pottering endlessly about (while 'tutting' quietly and continuously about her husband's ridiculous ways), would end up on the edge of smiling.

Although he was so totally at ease in the centre of his circle of male relatives and friends, Grandad also enjoyed the company of women. He admired and respected their special characteristics and secretly accepted, I think, that they were different not inferior. As a young man he had been something of a womanizer, and he greatly appreciated female beauty. Nellie was tiny, but Grandad's ideal of beauty was actually on a grander scale. 'The way she's growing, she'll be a strapping wench,' he said one day of me. And, once, describing our Great Aunt Margaret, his favourite sister, he painted a vivid picture of her dark good looks when young, ending up: 'She was a fine figure of a woman.'

I think he felt much the same about my mother. Even when relations between Gran and Mum were at their coolest, Grandad could seldom be pressed to become a party to the estrangement. When Mum went 'out the back' she would usually find a friendly word from Grandad if he was about. Even when she slyly picked great bunches of his treasured flowers without asking him, and hid them under her overall going along the side-way, his anger was of brief duration. 'Jean's been at your plants again,' Gran would tell him maliciously. 'Bloody woman!' he would roar. 'I'll tell *her* who's the head in this household.' But when they met again he'd have forgotten all except his pleasure at seeing this handsome daughter-in-law. 'Hello Jean. Nice clear morning. There'll be no rain today,' he'd say, or some such friendly nothingness.

It was always good to find Grandad in the garden. He would seldom be too busy, or too engrossed in his gardening or newspaper or book, to stop and 'converse'. Of course I knew that his orphaned grandsons, Pete and Ken, must be in some ways special to him, but I fancied that he also had a special place for me as the only girl in the house. Oddly, he never used my christian name when addressing me, although if he wanted me to run an errand for him, usually to change his library books again, he would call upstairs, 'Jean, is Phyll about?' Face to face, I was always 'gal' or 'pretty'. 'Hello gal' or 'How are you today, my pretty?'

He seemed to like my talkativeness – an attribute not always appreciated by Mum or the others. But I was also a willing, indeed eager, listener to any anecdote of his past life or any item of interest that caught his eye in the news. 'Listen to this, gal,' he'd say, and then sonorously declaim a paragraph or two from his paper. On days when we were on particularly close terms he would pat his bench and invite me to sit beside him instead of on the opposite one, and then, to mark our intimacy, get out his little tin of snuff and offer me a pinch.

Walter Noble travelled far in many senses from his parents' tied cottage and his deprived childhood in Suffolk. Yet his sons, four or five of whom were at least as, if not more, intelligent that he was, did not make such dramatic changes in their lives. Only one of the nine sons was led by his career to leave the place in which they were born and bred and, apart from the two killed in the Great War, the others clustered round the parental home in the south London 'village' throughout their lives. The extraordinary hold Grandad seemed to have over his sons was not however that of a dominating personality – Gran for all her quietness was the domineering parent – but rather of a powerful charm that ensnared us all.

7

Blunham

Not long after Joey's birth Mum found herself pregnant yet again. By means of gin, quinine, jumping down the stairs and similar traditional methods, she managed to abort the pregnancy. She was herself convinced that accidentally witnessing this experience induced in Wally – an otherwise most courageous boy – not only a lasting proclivity to faint at the sight of blood, but also an incurable distaste for rabbit. The foetus, raw and bloody-looking, 'came away' to flop on the floor when she was in the kitchen with him. He was then between four and five years old. Unfortunately, immediate ill-effects resulted from this abortion, and Mum soon after had to go to the Miller Hospital at Greenwich to see a gynaecologist. He told her she would have to come into hospital for an operation, and asked her where her home was. 'Blunham,' she answered. 'Blunham?' the doctor said in some amazement. 'Where is that?' 'Bedfordshire,' she said. Later, having got the position clear, he said to her, 'My dear young woman, you have three young children, don't you realize that now your home is where they and your husband are?'

At this time I was about three and a half, and Wally around five. Unknown to us, arrangements were set in motion for us children to be cared for while Mum went into the Miller. We were told we were going to Blunham, which delighted us for we had already had many happy summer days in Mum's Bedfordshire 'home'. Every summer for three or four weeks, sometimes more, we went on holiday with Mum to Granny Mann's. Dad, who during the good summer weather was usually working most of the daylight hours trying to earn as much as possible in overtime, would come down once or twice at weekends to see us.

One morning, too excited to notice that it was Dad who was with us instead of Mum, we got on the tram 'up to London' to catch the train from the terminus. At King's Cross Station Dad met Uncle Bob, my mother's brother, who was a porter there. He made a great fuss of us, of course, and told us to our even greater excitement that this time we were going to Blunham in the guard's van. Sure enough we were soon, not just squeezed, but firmly wedged into the guard's seat in one corner of the van. Busy with the chocolates and comics with which Dad and Uncle Bob had plied us before the train went off, we hardly had time to notice that Dad and Uncle Bob had disappeared. At every stop the guard or some new railway figure we assumed must be a new friend or 'uncle' greeted us cheerily and pushed more sweets or comics at us. When we got to Blunham Uncle Joe, another of Mum's brothers 'on the railway', was waiting to sweep us up in his arms and whisk us into his side-car to drive to Granny Mann's. What had happened to Dad and Mum? It was a puzzle, but not yet a worry because it was in our experience inconceivable that Mum, or Dad at least, would not be somewhere close by.

Tea was waiting for us at Granny Mann's, and a warm welcome from her, Auntie Rose (wife of Uncle Joe) and one or two villagers well known to us. We were admired, family likenesses noted and discussed (I was always said to be the image of 'Jenny', my mother, at any age I visited) and then, just as darkness had fallen, Uncle Joe said, 'Come on my ducks, we must be going.' Going where? For the first time that day anxiety seized hold of me and I began to ask, 'But where is Mummy?' My unease turned to panic when I realized that not only had Mum vanished, but any minute now I was to lose Wally too. He was to stay with Granny Mann, I was to go with Uncle Joe and Auntie Rose. They lived in the next village of Moggerhanger, and as we drove through the unknown darkness I began to cry. At Moggerhanger I continued to sob on

Uncle Joe's lap for what seemed, and may well have been, hours. Uncle Joe patiently rocked me all the while and repeated endlessly, 'Never mind, my ducks. Hush, my ducks. There, my ducks. Never mind. . . .' From time to time Auntie Rose showed signs of losing patience and suggested putting me up to bed. But Uncle Joe would have none of this, and holding me close in his arms eventually rocked me until I could sob no longer and fell asleep.

I lived with Uncle Joe and Auntie Rose that spring for about six weeks. Mum was in hospital for three, and then came down herself to convalesce at Blunham where I saw her on our Sunday visits there. After that first night I have no memory of unhappiness or tears at Moggerhanger except for one other evening when I howled again with earache and Uncle Joe, once again, showed the same patient lovingness.

The cottage at Moggerhanger was a long, two-storey building at right angles to the road. At the road end, the first room of the house was the village corner shop and sub-post office. Behind it was the parlour, in which a doorway opened onto the stairs which led to the two bedrooms above, one leading out of the other. Next to the parlour was the big, sloping-ceilinged scullery-kitchen, beyond that a lean-to and then the chicken shed. Opposite was a great wooden barn, and in between a pretty, typical country-cottage garden.

Uncle Joe and Auntie Rose, much to Joe's regret, had no children. While Joe worked on the railway, Rose ran the shop and sub-post office. When I arrived it was at first assumed that I could simply run around after Rose. But only a few days had passed before Auntie Rose realized that a lively three-and-a-half-year-old in the shop was more than she had bargained for. I was thrilled at the red letter box in the wall of the shop, and wanted Auntie Rose to unlock her side in the shop every few minutes to see if any more letters had been posted. Trying to cut the cheese with the wire cutter, measuring up sugar from the sack with the scoop and scales, buying and weighing my own sweets, and making my own bag to put them in from a twist of paper – all this seemed to me a source of endless pleasure and amusement. For Auntie Rose, used to a quiet and solitary life, it must have been unbearable.

As I had already started at the LCC kindergarten back in London, special arrangements were made for me to attend the infants' class of the village school. I was taken each day by a sort of relative – a niece of Auntie Rose – who lived at the pub opposite. Her name was Betty and although she was several years older than me we became close friends. I didn't mind going to school with her – she was in a different class, but protected me by the influence of her relationship. Now, all I can remember of the school is the playground at the front and the lavatories which were basically a row of buckets in a shed at the back. I was probably at school too little of the time I was at Moggerhanger for it to make much impression. Easter came, and during the holidays I was sent over to spend the day playing with Betty Osborne.

She was an only child and, although in many ways indulged by her parents, was left a great deal to her own devices. Her father had a smallholding at the back of the pub, which kept him busy, while her mother ran the pub itself. Betty had a donkey in the meadow at the back on which she gave me rides. She also had part of an old railway coach which had been converted into a little house for her to play in. We spent many happy hours together there, cleaning and tidying, setting the table and eating our meals, and sometimes, by special permission, sleeping there too. It was all very comfortable and utterly ours. We could play 'doctors and nurses' without risk of interruption, and it was here that I really awoke to the delights of this kind of sexual game, and of the physical pleasure, the tingling sensations, they could bring.

I also discovered the beauty of the countryside in spring. The head-spinning scent of the primulas bordering the Osbornes' small, green garden after a shower in the early evening. The joy of chasing a rainbow which looked as if it *must* end just behind the wall of the buildings across the road. The yellow of nearby woods, carpeted with a thousand wild daffodils. The scent of baskets full of cowslip heads.

Uncle Joe and Auntie Rose were militant teetotallers. They were also great makers of home-made wines. The low end of the flagstoned scullery was crammed with bottles full of all kinds of brews, including elderberry, parsnip, cherry, dandelion and cowslip. During my visit I was enlisted to play my part in collecting baskets full of dandelion heads and cowslips. The scullery floor was strewn with bowls and buckets and baskets filled with the yellow flower heads. As Aunt Rose went on with the process, the whole house was permeated with their sweet smell. Eventually bottles were filled and added to the store. Visitors were offered a glass or two of these nectars when they came. Dad, who found his wife's relatives a serious and sober lot, could always be persuaded to visit Uncle Joe on his brief trips to Blunham. To him it was an enormous joke that these confirmed teetotallers would not see that their home-made brews were often far more intoxicating than some of the 'alcoholic beverages' they were so against.

As time passed and I became more and more happily settled in this country paradise, I came to understand that Mum was in hospital. Auntie Rose persuaded me to collect flowers to send her, and I filled a box with green moss and embedded small bunches of primroses and violets in it. But at home or in hospital, Mum and London seemed far away, and I had no feelings of loss or longing to return to her. Uncle Joe adored having me, and I was fussed over and coddled far more than ever I was at home. Used to sharing love and possessions with my brothers, and always taking second place to Joey (because he was 'the baby'), I relished Uncle Joe's attention. He taught me how to collect eggs from the chickens' nest boxes, and how *not* to disturb a hen while it was laying. He showed me the great white owl that lived in the barn (I had refused to believe that any except 'brown owls' existed). He held me on his lap in the evenings and teased and flattered me, and told me stories. All the frustrated parent in him was lavished over me during that lovely spring.

On Sundays we spent most of the day at Blunham. Auntie Rose and Uncle Joe were both strongly Methodist, and both were in the choir of the Methodist Chapel in Blunham. We went over in the mornings, came back for lunch, then returned for tea at Granny Mann's and the evening service at the Chapel.

It was on one of these Sundays that I came across Mum again. There she was, sitting in a chair at Granny Mann's. To her chagrin (and Uncle Joe's pleasure no doubt) I treated her like a stranger and refused to leave Uncle Joe's side. But when the time came to go back to Moggerhanger all my repressed longings for her must have broken through. I cried and clung to her and begged to stay. It seemed even less fair that Wally was with her, while I had to go. On the Sundays that followed Mum had time to see how I had fared under Uncle Joe's doting care. She was not entirely pleased at my even perkier ways, and was saying before we left for home, 'She's been thoroughly spoilt. She'll have to change her ways when we get back to London again.' And indeed after we returned we had a hard time for a while, as she knew we would. I struggled to get from her the undivided love Uncle Joe had showered on me, and got many a slap before I settled down again to accept my place as one of three, instead of the one and only.

Perhaps because, in different ways, it was too disturbing to everyone, I never again stayed with Uncle Joe at Moggerhanger, although our annual visits to Blunham continued for some years more. Blunham, a not particularly pretty place, had a small collection of thatched cottages, two shops, a school, a charming old church in the centre and the plainer Methodist Chapel at its edge. The River Ouse wound round the edge of the village. We walked to it under an avenue of limes beginning opposite Granny Mann's cottage. This avenue led to 'the park', probably the squire's estate originally, but now open to use by the villagers.

Locally, the river was considered a treacherous one, with sudden depths and currents. But we were allowed to paddle at its edges, and fish for sticklebacks amongst the flowing reeds. We had happy picnics there, a short walk away from Granny Mann's cottage. Once, when Auntie Bertha and her three children were also with us, Mum was helping cousin Peggy and I to 'balance' along the low fence bordering the bank on one side. Peggy lurched, tried to clutch onto me, and I fell, tumbling down the bank into the thick bed of nettles beside the water. As I was wearing only a short dress and pants, my face, hands, legs, arms and thighs were exposed to the nettles' stings as I rolled helplessly down the bank. Mum, striving to avoid too many stings on her own legs, picked her way, cautiously but as quickly as she could, through the knee-high nettles, and pulled me out. The pain of the stings had transfixed me. I stood rigid unable to cry, to breathe, to move. First Mum shook me, then alarmed at my bluish face, gave it a stinging slap with her hand. I drew breath, began to bellow, and was immediately cuddled and cooed over and given all the warm sympathy that Mum poured upon any of us when we were hurt or ill.

We all hurried back to the cottage, Mum shouting out to the villagers we met on the way what had happened to cause my reddened skin and violent sobs. It was decided I needed to be swabbed with vinegar, and so I was. Half an hour later I was sent to buy myself sweets at the village shop. The worst of the stinging had gone but the rash showed clearly, and I could enjoy being the centre of the villagers' concern over my terrible experience (which by then everyone seemed to have heard of).

When Bertha and her children were also staying at Granny Mann's, the cottage was very full indeed. Granny Mann seemed not to mind although at other times she lived there alone. Upstairs under the thatch roof, there was only one bedroom. The stairs, which like Uncle Joe's were shut off from the kitchen-living room by a door at the bottom, led up into the one room above with its exposed beams, sloping ceiling and small dormer window. There were two double beds; Bertha and Mum slept in one, and we six children slept length-wise in the other.

Granny Mann slept in the room downstairs as she had done all those married years when her own children had, like us in our turn, shared the beds upstairs. We children seldom went into Granny Mann's bedroom but my memory of it is of a comfortable pinkish place with a high, curtained bed of four-poster design.

If Dad or Uncle Sid came down for the weekend Bertha or Jenny moved downstairs to share Granny Mann's bed, so that husband and wife could enjoy reunion in the double bed upstairs. It was not always easy on summer nights for us children to get to sleep so closely cramped together. I soon found, as I grew beyond the toddler stage, that my feet stuck out at the bottom (really the side of the bed) or that I would soon lose my share of the sheet, or my half of a pillow. But there was also an enveloping quiet and cosiness in the cottage. On Saturday nights the Salvation Army band assembled in the small space where the road widened outside the cottage, and their music floated in to us. How utterly safe our world seemed then in this happy timeless place.

Daily life was lived in the kitchen-living room with its old black range built into the far older oak-beamed fireplace, on each side of which were small inglenook seats. Granny Mann's long years of practice had perfected her knowledge of regulating the cooking temperatures of the old oven and range. Her creamy baked rice puddings, sprinkled with nutmeg, were ambrosia. Mum remembered that in her own childhood Grandad Mann came home every day to a boiled suet pudding, either as a meat course or, with jam or currants, as dessert. In those days Granny Mann also made the dough for her own bread twice a week but this was baked in the 'second oven' of the village bakery on the days it was lit for cake making.

There was no gas or electricity, and well-water was hand-pumped into a flat sink in the scullery. The scullery, as in many cottages of this age, was a later back extension built onto the main wall of the house. It was thatched and had small windows and the floor was red-tiled, but all kinds of baskets, strings and ropes, tools and utensils hung from the walls and beams and cluttered up corners everywhere so that it seemed more like a shed than anything. It smelt of vegetables, well-water and dampness. From the scullery a path down the tangled garden – neglected since Grandad Mann had died, but still producing fruit from overgrown gooseberry bushes, raspberry canes, apple, plum and greengage trees –

led to the earth closet. A wooden seat, scrubbed bone-white over the years, offered the choice of three different-sized holes to match different-sized bums. It was a relaxing place to sit in with a cousin, brother, or even a parent, on a sunny day. The hum of flies, and the buzz of other insect life in the trees shading the shed, the pungent but not unpleasant odour of mingled earth and faeces made it a pleasure to sit so long that one's bum stuck like a cork in the round wooden hole, unless by urgent need or bad luck one had been forced to use the big hole clearly provided for adult buttocks. Wandering back up the garden path it was easy to pick yet another plum or one of the huge, hairy and yellow 'dessert' gooseberries. If Granny Mann 'caught you', her scolding took a little of the sweetness off. She had the country woman's fear of 'too much soft fruit' eaten raw. She liked to set us to work picking the gooseberries from the prickly bushes for use in her puddings and for jam. We soon protested at this enforced labour, but she was tougher on us than our mothers were when she had the chance to be. She urged us on to fill our baskets, long after our enthusiasm had flagged.

Granny Mann was not born in Bedfordshire. She was one of the many children of a farm labourer born near Fakenham, Norfolk. Her own childhood had been brief and harsh. Her father was said to have fallen off a haywagon when drunk, breaking his neck and leaving her mother widowed with a great brood of children to rear as best she could. Granny Mann had some half-time schooling, and worked on the land, potato-picking and so on, from an early age to help the family economy. At thirteen she was sent from home to be nursery maid to an upper-class family. She met Grandfather Mann while still with this family and on a seasonal trip to their London house.

Grandfather Mann was born in Oxfordshire, near Banbury. He was the younger son of a wheelwright and carpenter, what his eldest son was many years later to describe to me as of 'good yeoman stock'. Grandfather Mann had also started work early. A joke of his, so my mother said, was that he had 'been at Oxford University'. He was a bootboy there. Ambitious, he joined the railways while still very young, and soon moved to London in pursuit of advancement. A job on the railways then offered many advantages which were highly valued – security, a uniform which saved on the cost of clothes, possibilities for promotion and at least some chance of a pension at retirement. He and Granny Mann moved to Blunham on his appointment as stationmaster there.

As a young man Grandfather Mann had indulged a taste for alcohol. Granny Mann married him only after a promise to give up drink, which he never transgressed. Even on his painful deathbed, fifty years later, he refused a sip of brandy: 'No, no, I promised Mary I wouldn't.' A radical politically, and an active Methodist, Grandfather Mann made a strong impression on his adopted village. He fought a continuous battle against encroaching farmers and landowners, when necessary leading gatherings of villagers to prevent any attempts at closing public footpaths. Dressed in his stationmaster's uniform of frock coat and top hat, his black shaggy beard round his face, he would advance, strike down the barrier and boom, 'I declare this footpath open!' At the Methodist Chapel, if dissatisfied with the volume of singing, he thought nothing of taking over, on God's behalf, and strode up and down the centre, waving his arms in encouragement, at the same time increasing the volume of his own powerful voice.

He was stern and strong-willed, so his eldest son, my Uncle Jack, told me, but he was also emotional and warmhearted. Uncle Jack, like several others of the Mann boys, was put to work on the railways too. Uncle Jack was placed at an early age as booking-clerk 'down the line'. He boarded out weekly and came home only at weekends. He told me ruefully one day of the embarrassment he suffered as a young adolescent each time he got off the train at Blunham. Invariably, down the platform he would see his father. Resplendent in his stationmaster's garb and long beard, tears streaming down his face, Grandfather Mann would advance towards him, arms spread wide, unashamedly sobbing out loudly, 'My boy! My boy!'

To Granny Mann, this splendid man had only one fault – his

untiring sexual appetite, which kept her pregnant almost continually through her fecund years. Wise from her experience of London life, perhaps she knew better than to reject his demands. When my mother complained soon after her wedding that marriage 'would be alright, if only I could keep him away from me', Granny Mann advised her: 'Never refuse him! If he doesn't get what he wants from you, he'll look elsewhere.'

After her husband's lingering death from cancer of the bowels, Granny Mann lived on alone at Blunham. She spent a large part of her day sitting behind the geraniums and other plants in her window, cutting and sewing furiously with her treadle machine. She undertook work for anyone in the village, running up dresses, pyjamas, sheets or curtains in a day if necessary. Her charges were acknowledged to be low to all, but no more than pride-saving tokens to those she felt too poor to pay. Her children were constantly chivvying her to charge more, and were aggrieved at the way she was imposed on, according to their way of thinking. But nothing could make her alter her prices. She 'wanted for nothing' herself, and 'these poor dears can't pay more'. Not surprisingly she was never without friends or visitors. Perhaps she was acting out as best she could the socialist ideals she knew her husband had held so dear, and had practised in his rather different (and not always, to her, comprehensible) ways.

8

Mum

Auntie Bertha, Mum and Auntie Pam were the last three of the eleven children Granny Mann had borne. Being the youngest children in a large family, the three sisters had in many ways a better time and a longer childhood than their older brothers and sisters. Grandad Mann had only of necessity, but with great reluctance, allowed his older daughters to go off 'into service', helping the rich in the unequal society he deplored. He was glad that the sacrifices asked of his elder children were not needed from the younger. Auntie Bertha was sent to an apprenticeship as a 'court dressmaker'. Auntie Pam was trained to teach. Mum – 'Jenny' at Blunham – was something of a problem; she was anaemic and failed to menstruate at all until she was eighteen years old. For this reason, she stayed longest at home, helping in the school as a 'pupil-teacher'.

There were disadvantages as well as advantages in being one of the younger members of the family. Granny Mann's hard life of heavy domestic work and incessant years of pregnancies and child-rearing made its mark on her. To her younger daughters she was never other than grey-haired, wrinkled and worn. Her smartest clothes, her 'Sunday best' of long black dress and 'Dora' bonnet, were hardly distinguishable from her equally sober navy-blue and brown dresses, covered by the ubiquitous printed cotton overall, of weekday wear. Although Mum was very close to the two sisters who were later to marry into the same family as herself, another disadvantage for her of coming next but last in a large family was that most of her elder brothers and sisters were more like uncles and aunts to her. They were fond of 'little Jenny', but there was not the same close bond as between children who grow up together.

By the time Mum had matured enough for it to be considered safe to send her from home – that is to say, at eighteen, when she at last began to menstruate – Auntie Bertha was already in London, employed as a seamstress on the staff of Ladywell Infirmary. This gave the Manns the idea of finding employment in a hospital for Jenny too. She obtained a post as nursing assistant in an asylum. It proved to be a traumatic experience which came to an end soon after she was attacked by a violent patient confined to a padded cell, who lifted her by the bun at the nape of her neck and held her swinging helplessly by it. The violence with which this patient, and others, were 'punished' by the martinet of a Sister shocked Mum almost as much as the attack itself.

Soon after, Auntie Bertha, who was something of a favourite with the Matron at Ladywell, arranged for Mum to go there too, but on the nursing side. This was an improvement on the asylum, but after the Great War started and the infirmary became a military hospital it became even better. Nursing young men, basking in their flattery and praise, with a score of invitations to choose from for each brief hour off duty, pretty Jenny, her large brown eyes a striking contrast in the luminous pallor of her anaemic face, found life more fun than it had ever been. Her gentleness and kindly disposition made her a good nurse. But the attention and flattery surrounding her could hardly fail to turn her head a little. Her seventeen-inch waist, elegantly emphasized by the starched white belt round it, her fine, gold-flecked brown hair, her eyes and skin, her classic profile were appreciated fully and loudly commented on as she walked the wards. She became a little vain, capricious, proud.

There was much of this vanity and capriciousness still in her when we were young. Susceptible, as children are, we too became proud of her good looks, and perhaps all the more attached to her because of her unpredictable moods which could change from a smiling gaiety to an anger ending in swift, sharp slaps for all of us for some 'naughtiness' – half the time we hardly knew what for. Cooped up in the tiny kitchen, with three toddlers under her feet while she tried to 'get on' with her work, she must often have looked back with longing to her salad days at the hospital. But she did her best to amuse us. On sunny days she would give us a 'picnic' lunch by opening up the scullery window and using the window-sill as a table at which we sat on the wooden bench Dad had made for us. Then we could 'feed the birds' by throwing out crumbs onto the corrugated roof of the shed below us, until they became a sludgy mess in the 'dips' of the iron. When it became too messy Mum would climb out and stand on the roof, sweeping the sludge over the edge to fall into the garden below, all the while keeping an eye on us looking out and begging to join her on the roof. Every day after lunch she insisted on a 'few minutes' quiet'. We looked at our books, or sat drawing at the table, while she put her feet up on a stool and tried to 'lose herself'. This quiet time, which seemed endlessly long, was in fact often no more than a few minutes. For a second or so she dozed off, then opening her eyes again said, 'There, I lost myself. Now let's get ready to go out.' These moments of absolute peacefulness and quiet refreshed us all.

One afternoon when we were still very young we didn't go out. She said, 'A man is coming to see us.' He arrived, we were told to sit – and stay there – against the wall, while Mum pulled out a chair and sat down in the middle of the room. The man put an overall round Mum's shoulders, let down the silk-soft, streaky hair, and started to cut. We began to cry. As the swathes of hair came off, so our fear grew greater and our sobs louder. I do not know why we found this so upsetting, but the barber and Mum seemed more amused than angered by the noise we were making. Of course we soon got used to the new 'bobbed' mother. The severed hair was tied into a coil, and then shoved in the dresser drawer which was always crammed with bits of wool, scissors, broken oddments and button-tins, odd tattered books or documents. Tossed in this jumbled mass, the hair gradually lost its silky sheen and became a messy tangle. But it was some years before Mum had the heart to throw it out.

As time went by, like the shine on her hair, Mum's gaiety seemed to slowly decrease. She no longer sang songs in her warbling, choir-trained soprano as she worked in the scullery and we played in the kitchen. Across the way, we could sometimes still hear the singing of Mrs Jepson, our 'back neighbour', but Mum no longer took up the song and joined in a duet with her. She more often looked worried and preoccupied, and her relationship with Dad frequently became cold or openly quarrelsome. The depression years were beginning to bite. Money, or the lack of it, became a source of nagging anxiety; shopping, once a pleasure and amusement, became a nightmare from which awakenings were rarer, even in the summer months.

On Saturdays we usually walked to Lewisham, pushing the pram with Joey in it, to do the weekly shopping. Along the crowded street with shops on one side, and stalls on the other, we enjoyed comparing prices, keeping an eye open for a bargain, and urging Mum to 'look at this' or 'please get some of those'. But as Mum came to enjoy these Saturday afternoons less she found me, in particular, very trying: 'Your worrying drives everything out of my mind! I can't think *what* I want.' If she could, she preferred to take just Wally to help her, and to leave Joey and me behind.

Not much later, Wally and I were given a list and sent off on our own to Lewisham because things were 'so tight', as Dad would say, that no more than the basic requirements could possibly be bought, no matter how cheap or how much of a bargain they were. Once, walking home again (fares to go on the tram were an extravagance we had to forgo at such times), Wally or I managed to drop the basket, which was quite heavy for us to carry a whole mile. To our dismay we had broken the two-pound jar of cheap grade jam from the market which then cost sixpence. Anxious and upset, we hurried home to tell Mum. To our misery she did not, as we had expected, shout or hit us in her quick-tempered way. She just threw her pinny up over her face, sat down in her chair and sobbed. Desperate to console her, we declared that we didn't care a bit about not having any jam on our bread. She cried even harder.

Things were not usually so bad in the summer months when Dad almost always had work. In fact, sometimes they were almost carefree again. Mum used to pay off the debts she had built up in the winter, store up coal, and pay larger amounts each week to the loan clubs and Provident clothing club which would help at Christmas or birthdays. Dad, unfortunately, was by temperament incapable of saving for a 'rainy day'. He must have known that bad days with no work would come next winter, yet as soon as he was on overtime 'bringing in the money' he was spending it too. To pinch and scrape all summer in order to do the same in winter too was, to his mind, admitting that life was not worth living. So we would be given half-crowns to spend, great bags of assorted sweets would be brought home for us on Friday night, Mum would get 'presents' of jewellery or money for a new dress or coat. This kind of extravagant, impulsive spending on us Mum did not mind. What she resented was the equal largesse and generosity Dad lavished at weekends on his friends and relatives at the pub.

During these good summer months, however, Mum would be taking us to Lewisham again and enjoying the pleasures of buying 'spec' fruit to make jam, 'setting us up' with new plimsolls or clothes, hunting out cut-price wool and sale-reduced bits of material, and 'lashing out' on tea-time treats for Dad of crab or salmon. Then one day the gypsy would turn up again on the corner near the Clock Tower with her great basket of lavender. Mum would stop, buy a bunch and sigh. 'That's a sure sign your Dad won't be working much longer.' Of course, she always hoped that, this year, she would be proved wrong. 'Poor Mum,' I said on the way home one day and, hanging onto her arm, full of love for her. 'Poor Mum, you have such a hard time because of us. But when I'm grown I'll buy you everything you want, even a fur coat for the winter!' She looked down at me with affection but answered laconically, 'When you're grown up, you'll be doing the same as I am now – worrying where the next penny is coming from to feed *your* kids, and how to keep their feet dry, never mind fur coats.'

The hard years were taking their toll of Mum's beauty. Her eyes, always deep-set, seemed to be sinking deeper into her face. She told us it was because she cried so much now. Her fine skin, neglected, began to wrinkle and coarsen and the long narrow nostrils of her large but well shaped nose developed a wet and pinkish tinge as if she always had a cold. More anxious about getting enough for us to eat (and for Dad too because he was the breadwinner), she neglected her own needs. Her teeth began to cause her trouble. The dentist recommended taking them out. She came home, bloody-mouthed from two afternoon sessions during which all her upper and lower teeth were extracted. For months afterwards, tiny slivers of tooth or bone would ooze up through the gums. Not yet middle-aged she embarked on the misery of wearing her first set of ill-fitting dentures. Her tiny waistline, of which she had been so proud, had now thickened and her hips spread – the result, in her own view, of the fanatical tight-corsetting she had imposed on herself to conceal her pregnancies as much as possible. All the same, with the help of the false teeth, ten minutes' work with the curling iron, lipstick and powder, and her newest dress (bought when Dad was 'flush'), she could still look handsome.

It was not only the poverty that was wearing Mum down, changing a kindly and gay disposition into one of bitterness and dejection. Auntie Pam's death was a great blow, but only a year later worse was to follow. I arrived home first from school one day, a few minutes before a telegram arrived. It was for Mum. She stood in front of the fireplace as she opened it, and then collapsed into a frenzy of sobs and howling such as I had never heard before. 'Tell me what's the *matter,* Mum,' I begged. 'Granny Mann's died.' She forced out the words between her paroxysms. I knew that Granny Mann had been ill and was being cared for devotedly at Blunham by Bertha. That she had now died did not in itself shock me, or indeed have much meaning. But Mum's terrible grief was another matter. I was eight years old, and I tried my best to console her. 'Never mind, Mummy. She's with God now, so you should be happy, not sad!' 'I don't care if she's with God or not. *I've* lost her. I've lost the dearest and best mother a girl ever had,' gasped the shaking, rocking bundle in the chair. It was my turn to suffer a shock. My mother's response seemed wrong; to deny God's prior right to Granny Mann was surely not far short of wickedness.

A year or two later, as hardships continued to press on our little household, I began to be less convinced of God's precedence. The year following Granny Mann's death was a hard and sad one for us all. Uncle Bert, who had never been strong after the rigours of his war service on the Russian front, began to go downhill quickly after Pam's death. He was advised to try a cruise and went to Australia employed as a steward on a liner for six months. On his return he went off to a sanatorium. He hated it and discharged himself home, where for a while he tried to keep the sanatorium's open-air routine by sleeping in a tent Dad put up in the garden for him. Haemorrhages became a commonplace which whipped him off to Grove Park Hospital from time to time. Always, when he could, he escaped to his home again. He was still sharing the downstairs back room with his twin brothers, Harold and Bern, who were by then young men of about eighteen or nineteen, and so the public health authorities became increasingly a threatening influence. We were all even more on guard than usual to the dangers of letting anyone into the house. Or even of admitting to any stranger on the doorstep that anyone they asked for was in.

An urgent call from Bern, who was at home that day, caused Mum to hurry downstairs to the sick-room where Bert had been lying, growing weaker, for some weeks. Another haemorrhage had begun. It increased as Mum arrived and poor Bert, beginning to choke in his own blood, sat up in bed. 'Lie down, my dear. For God's sake lie down,' Mum cried out as his life pumped out of him. We came home from school to find him dead. It was Mum, again, who mopped up the pools of blood, stripped the bed and laid him out. A day or two later when all was done, and Uncle Bert was in his coffin, Gran took Pete and Ken in to see their dead father and

Mum asked us three children upstairs if we wished to see him.
Wally and Joe would not go. Curiosity, more than bonds of
affection, drew me to say 'yes'. Mum took me into the darkened
room, which was suffused with an unfamiliar sweet smell. She
removed the square of muslin covering Bert's face. His skin was
pale yellow and waxen. His thick black hair no longer fell over
one side of his forehead but lay smooth against his crown. 'He looks
beautiful,' I said, which, as it was meant to do, pleased my mother,
and no doubt everyone else in the family when she told them. I was
no longer so innocent as I had been a year before when Granny
Mann died; I did not finish my thought out loud: 'But it's not
Uncle Bert any more.'

Sadly, one good thing about Bert's death was that it eased the
sleeping arrangements in the overcrowded house. Wally was getting to be a big boy, and for some months Mum had been making
up a bed for him on an armchair-bed in the kitchen. Joey and I
still shared the single bed behind the curtain. Wally went first into
Mum and Dad's double bed and was half-wakened and half-
carried down the stairs to the kitchen when Mum and Dad's bedtime came round. This was not very satisfactory but neither, to
Mum, was the alternative of Wally being kept up until she and
Dad were ready for bed. Soon after Uncle Bert's death, Dad (after
some nagging from Mum) persuaded Gran to give up the big, front
bedroom she had slept in all her married life. She and Grandad
went into the small back bedroom downstairs, and her old room
became virtually a dormitory for the 'boys' – Joey and Wally,
cousins Peter and Ken, and Bern and Harold the young, twin
uncles (until their marriages soon after). This left only me – and
the bugs – still sharing Mum and Dad's room.

With Auntie Pam dead, Auntie Bertha thirty miles away from
London and relations with her mother-in-law cool and often
hostile, Mum would have been isolated and lonely but for the good
friend she found in our neighbour 'Jordan'. This small, prematurely white-haired, generous-natured woman was a widow. She
had married her dead sister's husband at least partly in order to

act as stepmother to her sister's two sons, only to find herself a few
years later alone with these two stepsons plus two more of her own.
She supplemented her small pension with the earnings from long
days of washing and charring for the 'nobs' at Blackheath. She had
the humour and wit of a cockney, but was in fact like Mum a
country girl by birth. She had been sent away to 'service' from her
village in Cornwall while still a girl. In her own eyes, her early
experience in 'service' had hardened her, and she was a constant
source of strength and encouragement to my mother who, Jordan
seemed to feel, was less strongly equipped for life's hard knocks.

Over the years Mum and Jordan became as close as sisters,
sometimes worked together, went shopping at sales together, and
invariably attended the same weekly meetings and annual outings
of the local Women's Institute. Yet, oddly, they continued for years
to pay lip service to the ideal of 'keeping themselves to themselves'
(as neighbours should) by the device of continually using surnames
for each other and to each other's children. They only took the final
leap into the intimacy of using first names – 'Lil' and 'Jean' – when
all their children had grown up and moved out of the parental
homes and they were able to enjoy leisurely afternoon hours in
each other's kitchens reminiscing with sighs and laughter over their
past times together.

Jordan knew when things were toughest next door because then
more often than was usual one of us children would be sent over
the fence in the garden to 'ask Jordan if she can lend us a scrape of
flour' – or it could be sugar, or tea, or an onion or even half-a-
crown – 'until the end of the week'. It was always at times like this
that we would hear Jordan calling up to our scullery window,
'Noble! Are you there? Send one of the kids down a minute. . . .'
Over the fence she would hand us a newly baked bread pudding, a
jar of jam she would insist was 'a bit over' from some she had made
or been given herself. Her bread puddings were the most delicious
I have ever tasted, fatty and spicy, crisply browned on the outside,
yet deliciously soggy inside.

Although so good and so cheerful to us, Jordan was often a

tough mother to her own two young boys (but not to her nearly-grown stepsons). Sometimes the sound of her sons' howls, as Jordan chased them round the house beating them with their dead father's walking-stick, upset us all. Mum would be solemnly enjoined to 'warn Jordan' that Dad – or Grandad – was threatening to go to the 'Cruelty' if they heard her at it again. She was always sorry herself after her outbursts but, as she would say, it was hard bringing up boys alone. 'When I come home tired after a day's washing and they've done nothing I told them to and then they start acting about, I just seem to go mad.'

For a while, when times were grimmest, Mum and Jordan joined forces to earn an extra shilling or two. As an ex-nurse Mum was expert at laying out the dead, and people got to know this in the neighbourhood. With Jordan as her assistant, it was not a hard way of earning an occasional five shillings even if a somewhat macabre occupation for two young housewives. Even in the face of death Jordan could not resist making the best of the situation. Turning grim reality into a joke is, after all, no new way to keep the flag of the human spirit flying. After these sudden calls, Jordan would invariably have some tale to tell of corpses who gave them a shock by some unexpected movement like putting an arm out or round them. These experiences became gruesomely humorous stories when Jordan told and retold them to us and our relatives.

Jumble sales were another source of both profit and amusement to Mum and Jordan. They went together to any they heard about within walking distance. They went early enough to ensure their place near the head of the queue, waiting for the door to open, and they always kept close together. Serious arguments could develop between rival potential buyers at 'jumbles'. By sticking with each other Jordan and Mum ensured mutual support over claims between strangers and either of them over who had got hold of what first!

Sales at the big stores in Lewisham, Catford, Peckham Rye and Woolwich were excuses for something almost as enjoyable as the annual outing of the Women's Institute to the seaside. On the trams going and coming back from these expeditions their hilarity and noisiness went beyond the bounds of politeness. Ribald teasing of the conductor, together with the flirtatious attempts at 'getting away' with cheating over fares, drew the attention of all the tram's passengers to these 'loud' women. It was not the kind of behaviour that Dad or the other Noble men would have approved of from their women, though they would no doubt have been amused to observe such vulgarity in others not connected with them. In fact, Mum would not have dared behave in such a way if Dad had been around. And neither would Jordan, even though she had known Dad when he was still a boy and she, as a young girl, had come to visit her sister next door. They liked and respected each other, were always on friendly terms, but at the same time maintained a suitably polite distance between them. Probably Dad realized what a prop Jordan was to Mum. Certainly, those dark years would have been harder still to bear without Jordan, always sympathetic, ever striving to help Mum 'see the funny side of things'.

9

Outings and Adventures

The centre of our world at first was, of course, 49. Its main boundaries were roughly triangular. On one side Lee High Road (the
main road leading to Lewisham and 'London'), on the other the
Manor Park (known to Gran as the 'recreation ground'), and on
the third, behind us, the Quaggy. Beyond this small area, we knew
the names of streets and places but not, as a rule, those of the people
who lived there. As we grew older we began to explore further and
further beyond our own streets. We were encouraged to do this,
especially during school holidays, because it got us 'out of the way'
for a change and gave not only those in 49 but also the other residents of the road a bit of peace from our noise. Dad, who never
took a bus or tram anywhere he could reasonably walk, knew the
streets for several miles around as well as, indeed probably better
than, he knew the back of his hand. He could give detailed direc-
tions of how to reach some distant park (sign-posted entirely by the
names of the pubs en route). From an early age we got to know the
parks within walking distance of us when Mum, briefed by Dad,
took us to them for picnics. By the time we were considered big
enough to go off on our own, we knew the way as well as Dad did.

My own first adventure beyond our immediate boundaries
ended badly. I was about three years old and, having been given a
penny, went off to spend it at 'Burt's', the shop 'round the corner'
in Brightfield Road – or so Mum and Dad happily believed for a
while. My own intention, however, was to find the little tea-shop
in the park which also sold sweets. Something about this tea-shop

was always attractive to me. It had a Wendy House air about it which made a visit there for an ice or sweets – even better a cup of tea and a cake to eat at the little tables – a particular treat. I found my way to the shop all right. This was a simple enough matter of crossing our road, climbing up the slope of Aislibie Road (which was almost opposite) then turning left along Old Road (running behind and parallel to the present Lee High Road) and entering the gates of the park by the elegant, eighteenth-century Manor House, which had become the local library. A few yards down, past flower-beds and the avenue of giant plane trees, opposite the great elm beneath which crocuses flowered in profusion in spring, and between the public lavatories and the 'shelter', was the shop.

Preoccupied no doubt by my purchase, I turned the wrong way on coming out of the shop and unwittingly began to wander in the wrong direction for home. It slowly dawned on Mum and Dad that I should by now have been back. A quick search outside showed no sign of me. All Dad's worst fears for my safety grew large, but he refused to show his alarm and it was Mum, suddenly panic-stricken, who rushed off to the police station to report my disappearance. Meanwhile a woman who knew Mum and us children by sight had noticed me wandering in the streets on the 'foreign' side of the park. She did not know where we lived, but she had some idea it was 'on the other side' of the park, not her side. She took my hand and came back to Old Road. Once there I knew the way to our house again.

Mum was still wandering around asking if anyone had seen me, having been told at the police station to come back again if I had not turned up in an hour or so. It was Dad who took me in from 'the lady', thanked her politely, and fiercely grabbed hold of me. He did not hit me, but when he shut the front door his rough handling as he pushed me upstairs hurt as much as if he had. So did his angry voice as he told me what a bad, what a wicked, girl I was. Until then Dad's anger had largely been a threat of Mum's ('I shall tell your Dad when he comes home!'). This time the storm, heralded as always by the lightning flash in his blue eyes, had

broken over my own head. Before we reached the kitchen door I
was sobbing hard, but so great was Dad's fury at the anxiety I had
caused him he would still have nothing to do with me. Again I was
shoved roughly up the half-flight of stairs to our bedroom, pushed
inside and told to stay there. Such a punishment, such a complete
cutting-off of Dad's affection, was unknown to me. My sobs
increased to hysteria as I flung myself at the door which I could,
but dare not open. Unlike Dad, bottling his fears up at home,
Mum's walking about had drained off some of the tension created
in her by my brief disappearance. Relief and love were her overwhelming reactions on returning home and hearing my screams.
She bounded up the stairs to me, furious with Dad for what he had
done, and carried me down from the bedroom. Back in the kitchen
calmness returned, and I was persuaded to explain the how and
why of these first steps towards independence.

As we grew older we began to know the parks and open spaces
round us more intimately. Each had their special attractions, so
that discussions the night before an excursion could be prolonged
and bitter. I never got lost again after that first early experience,
but perhaps this was because I was not encouraged to go off on my
own. Mum and Dad insisted that I should 'go with the boys' or, if
it was somewhere very local, with one or other of my girl friends.
I liked going with the boys and their friends, but they weren't
always so pleased at having me tacked on to them, and even less if
I wanted to bring a girl friend with me too.

Mountsfield Park, near Catford, was favoured by the boys
because of its superior playground of mechanical ironwork – slides,
roundabouts, rockers – and good cricket facilities. I was not keen
on either of these and always apprehensive of the foreign 'gangs' of
boys we could run into there who seemed more often than not
spoiling for a fight. My favourite was beautiful Greenwich Park
which had steep hills to climb, 'wild' areas where the softest,
feathery-flowering grasses under the gigantic Spanish chestnuts
made idyllic picnic spots, elegant flower gardens and attractive
tea-houses and ice-cream kiosks. This was one of Mum's favourites

too, and at least once or twice a year she would come with us. Apart from our Sunday morning outings the only time the men of the household joined us on outings was on bank holidays. After the pubs had closed in the afternoon they would, good-humoured with beer, take us and their wives over to the fair at Blackheath.

One birthday, one of the boys was given a tent, and after this we grew more ambitious in seeking new places to 'camp' for the day. Then, as now, park-keepers, whether the blue-uniformed kind of the 'Royal' park at Greenwich or the brown-hued 'Council' men, did not look kindly on the pitching of tents in their domains. We had to head out of London to find the freedom we needed.

A walk from Lee to the Sidcup by-pass was about a mile. Sandwiches, cakes and lemonade were the 'food' stores I had to carry. Wally or Joey would take the tent, Peter and Ken the cricket bats, stumps and ball and their own food provided by Gran. Occasionally one of the boys' friends would be specially favoured to come with us. Less often, in a soft-hearted moment, Wally – unchallengably in charge – would agree to one of my friends coming along. But most often it was just the five of us, with me the only girl. Not far after the beginning of the Sidcup by-pass, beyond the school and firms' sports grounds on one side and the new and, according to Dad, 'jerry-built' houses springing up like a mushroom crop on the other, we came to 'real' fields. One belonged to the Express Dairy Company and had cows grazing in it. We might play around there for a while, for it had a clear little stream going through it, to fish and paddle in. In the spring, before it was warm enough to picnic or camp, we came to this same field carrying jam jars with string handles and nets to catch frogs' spawn.

On the other side of the by-pass was the second field, bounded on its second side by the railway embankment. Here we could pitch our tent and make our camp undisturbed. One year, on a lovely sunny day which was also Joey's birthday, Mum had arranged to come and join us, bringing with her a special picnic tea suitable for the occasion. When she came, to our surprise and joy, Auntie Bertha was with her. She had arrived on one of her unannounced day trips to London to see us. Her contribution to the birthday tea was a large tin of peaches which we ate out of our cups, before drinking Mum's lukewarm tea brought in bottles. The birthday cake for Joe was a large creamy sponge cake – Mum had got it cheap because it was 'stale' and the cream was slightly sour. We had, from long familiarity with 'stale cakes', acquired a taste for this particular flavour of slightly sour cream, and we did not consider it any the worse for that.

Sometimes we went even further afield to camp for the day on Chislehurst Common. This was too far to walk and so we could only go there when flush enough to pay the train fare two or three stations down the line on the Southern Railway. We almost lost our tent on one occasion. Happily lazing about in or around the tent in the birch woods of the common, we were set upon by a group of three or four boys a year or two older than any of us. They pestered us for a while, pulling out tent pegs and scuffling with the boys. I soon became uneasy and begged Wally to pack up the tent so that we could go off somewhere else. Sensibly, he refused to move until the boys had gone away. But when we had taken down the tent and were ready to move they reappeared from the woods. This time it seemed their intentions were even more aggressive; they were intent on making off with our now neatly packaged tent. A fight developed between Wally and the biggest boy on their side. I began to cry (to Wally's great fury for it made more obvious the always slightly shameful fact of having a girl 'tacked on').

As the fight grew fiercer, I got worse, begging Wally to hand over *everything* 'and let's just go'. The scene became more chaotic as the other boys began to spar about too, but slowly the strangers came to see that Wally's obstinacy was not easily overcome. It was getting late, and the sun dappling the wood was mellow as we at last began to pull out, carrying our stuff, and still sporadically under attack. In a final effort to break us the marauders picked up Ken, the youngest and slightest member of our party, and threw him into a gorse bush. At that time he happened to be holding the treasured tent, but despite the agonizing prickliness of the bush he still clung on. We pulled him out. The other boys, perhaps having already gone further than their own limits of acceptable aggressiveness, or possibly impressed by little Ken's stoicism, made off. As for us, we were all used to Wally's dogged courage in protecting our interests. It was Kenny's heroism that was unexpected and amazing.

It is clear to me now that Wally had no real choice. He could not have faced Dad and the 'men' at home if he had returned without the tent. The worst punishment the other boys could have inflicted on him in a fight was less than the shame of having to admit defeat to Dad and the others. They would not have punished him for losing the tent, but they would have mocked him. All the way home we talked over the events that had, in fact, ruined our day. By the time we came to retell them at home they had assumed an epic grandeur. As I told of the long struggle, Wally's tenacity, Peter and Joey's steady supporting actions and Kenny's unexpected bravery, Wally interrupted. He was pleased at my good account of him to Dad but it was also necessary to conceal his pride. 'And,' he said, with as much contempt as he could muster, '*she* just cried!'

Most of our expeditions were less dramatic than that long day at Chislehurst. Some days were good, and the sun shone on us. Others were dull and boring, and we found it difficult to spin out the time before setting off back home. After the trouble of making our picnic lunch, we knew that Mum was not likely to give us a warm welcome if we arrived home early. If it rained, sitting about in damp and dreary park shelters, or even our tent, soon became tedious. We ended up quarrelsome, dejected and cold. On those high days and holidays when Mum took us out the weather had less power to make or mar our day. Perhaps this was because when Mum was with us we were going to places where indoor attractions were likely to be near if the weather 'turned on us'. Or maybe she just could change our plans more easily or, since she came only at times when we were better off (otherwise she would not have been taking us out anyway), she could take us into a café for a cup of tea and a cake until things improved.

With Mum we often went further afield, so there was also the
pleasure of the journey there and back by tram. In another way,
however, rides on the tram were a doubtful treat. We were all constantly in dread of being sick, even though we also found exciting
their noisy clanking and whining; their swinging and rocking
motion; their occasional bursts of violent speed. A journey seldom
went by without one or other of us having to go to the back to hang
over the curved bay ready to vomit onto the receding track. Mum,
although out of habit complaining, was amazingly tolerant about
all this. She came to the back too, if vomiting seemed imminent,
and chatted away with the conductor while keeping one eye on
the green-faced child leaning out. Cousin Peter was particularly
prone to these attacks of nausea brought on by tram journeys,
but they were liable to overcome any one of us. The nausea
tended to be infectious – one started off another. We went by
tram 'up to London' for trips to St Paul's, to the Horse Guards or
the Houses of Parliament and, our greatest favourite in London,
the Tower.

Less far away, but also popular and regular, were the outings to
Woolwich Free Ferry where we rode back and forth across the grey
waters a dozen times or more while Mum went to look at the shops.
Closest to home, and reached by the bus from Lee to Blackheath,
were the long lovely days at Greenwich. These, because of the bus
route, began where we got off the bus at the south-east corner of the
park. From there we could find our way leisurely across the park
until we reached the Royal Observatory, where Mum would sit
for a while to admire the view and 'get back her breath', and we
would prance around trying, as always, unsuccessfully to 'read' the
time on the twenty-four-hour clock, stand with one foot on each
side of the white painted line marking the meridian, or roll and
chase each other down the hill which fell towards the Queen's
House, flanked by the Naval College and, beyond them, the
Thames.

If the weather was good we would soon be on our way again

down through the tree-covered hillside path curving round the base of the Observatory, and then on to the avenue lined with ancient Spanish chestnuts leading towards the great iron gates nearest Greenwich Pier. The atmosphere of the seaside seemed to greet us as we reached the exit. Through the gateway we would see the stalls selling their shrimps and cockles, sweets and ices, balloons and funny hats and souvenirs. We had already looked up the times of high tide in the paper, so we had some idea of how much 'beach' we would find on reaching the pier.

Walking along the riverside path in front of the Naval College we looked out for a sheltered and sandy spot on the shingle, preferably against steps or the river wall, on which to spread our pitch. Paddling; buckets and spades; watching the boats, big and small, appear and disappear round one bend of the wide, grey waters; picnics on the 'beach'; all the pleasures of a day at the seaside were ours for the price of a penny bus ride. It was a much rarer occasion for us to use Greenwich Pier to catch a boat down the river to the 'real seaside' of Southend or Margate. But at Southend once – it happened to be another day when Auntie Bertha was with us – I remember that I lost a brand new straw hat which, as we walked along the pier to get the boat home, blew off my head and sailed distantly away to land on the mud below. In retrospect at least, days at Greenwich Pier are the ones most remembered, ending in a journey home, tired but content.

If, as we sat at Wolfe's statue looking down on Greenwich's skyline of college buildings and cranes, the weather was not so encouraging we could always change our plans and go yet again to the museum and pore over Nelson's relics, the models of boats and paintings of Britain's naval glories. Or go into the College and look up again, in surprised incomprehension rather than wonder, at the famous 'painted hall'.

Walking back up the hill through the park was not quite as enjoyable as coming down at midday. On the way back the hill seemed steeper, the distances longer, but something about those soft green slopes of sweet-smelling grasses, majestic trees, fine vistas and graceful buildings could still give pleasure to the eyes feasting on them, even when our feet and legs were weary. Mum, being a country girl, enjoyed the green, the trees, the flowers as much as we did. Indeed she probably taught us to enjoy them so much. She always had interest to spare for a 'new' kind of grass or a bunch of daisies or a daisy-chain, an acorn still in its cup, a new glossy-coated chestnut. She knew the names of most trees and, where she didn't, went over – or sent one of us – to ask a keeper as soon as she saw one.

We always got home before it was dark: we had to be home before Dad got in. Not that he minded us being out (with Mum, at any rate) in darkness. The point was that the table must be laid for his tea when he came in. Even if we were out on our own, the same rule applied. As the picnic food invariably got eaten up early in the day we had an extra incentive to get back home in good time. But anyway our tea had to be eaten and cleared away before Dad arrived. His own place was laid, fresh and neat on the tablecloth half-folded to cover just the end he ate at. 'If we don't hurry, your Dad will be in,' set us all moving rapidly homewards. It never occurred to us to ask 'Does that matter?' Like so many of the rules governing our little lives it was beyond question.

10

Prayers for Pleasures

At one corner of Lampmead Road where the trams swayed and hummed along Lee High Road on their way to Lewisham clock tower and, beyond that, London, was the off-licence. It was the first in a short row of shops which included Mr Martin's, the draper, Mr Baxter's, the butcher, a sweet shop and, overlooking the Quaggy, one of Dad's favourite pubs, The Duke. Close by was the small cinema where we went to Saturday morning pictures and, almost opposite, the cottage where Gran grew up.

On the other corner of Lampmead Road were the almshouses, a row of two-storey Victorian dwellings which belonged to the Merchant Taylors. In the patch of grassed ground behind the almshouses a small red-brick chapel had been built at the same time, no doubt intended mainly for the convenience of the residents of the almshouses who, like Jordan's nearly blind mother, had secured a place there.

By the time I became aware of it the chapel was used by other local residents as well as those living in the almshouses. The parish church of St Margaret's was up in Blackheath. It was a fashionable place of worship for the Blackheath middle classes. In comparison, Boone's Chapel was more like a missionary outpost of the parish where the rector's voluntary workers came to do good with the Lee villagers on whom curates also learnt their craft.

Gran and Grandad never went to church. Unlike the old people who lived in the almshouses they were free of the moral pressures exerted by visits from churchworkers; they always gave us children the impression that at their age they were excused from further religious obligations. Their sons, once adult, never went either, except Dad who in special circumstances could be cajoled to put in an appearance. Mum, who had grown up in a deeply religious Methodist family, enjoyed being able to pop along to 'chapel'. The fact that it was not a non-conformist denomination did not trouble her. I suppose she believed in God out of upbringing and habit, but she was not a seriously religious woman. On the whole it was the social pleasures of church-going which drew her along: the chance for a word or two with friends and neighbours; the chance to sing; the chance to sit back and remember the Sundays of her own childhood.

I can't remember when I first went myself to Boone's Chapel, but it was probably soon after I had started going to Sunday school. By nine or ten I was considered old enough to go on my own and, as Mum's bouts of low spirits increased and she came less often, I sometimes did. But I much preferred it when Mum came too and together we could enjoy dressing ourselves up. Not that this amounted to much other than, for Mum, a slick of powder and lipstick and perhaps a new feather in an old hat or, for me, putting on the latest find from a jumble which we persuaded ourselves we had succeeded in making 'as good as new'.

One event which could be counted on to ensure Mum's attendance was the news that Wally (or any of the boys in their time) was to sing a solo. All of them, as they reached about eight years old, joined the choir; the chief attraction was the uncertain amount of cash they would get from the collections at certain points in the church year. Not surprisingly they took the religious side of their churchgoing lightly, and fidgeted and nudged and muttered out of the sides of their mouths to each other during the service. Some evenings they could be seen struggling against an attack of the giggles, or surreptitiously guiding a sweet into their mouths during the lessons or sermon, ducking as low as they dared in their pews to avoid the disapproving glances of the men in the choir who kept watch on them. Too much misbehaviour could mean temporary banishment at a subsequent service, somewhere out of sight to take a turn at pumping the organ.

Being in the choir was indeed a mixed blessing. Mum and Gran had to keep at them to make sure they turned out regularly for the twice-weekly evening choir practice. They also had to make sure the boys only occasionally played truant from morning and evening services on Sundays. The combination of the carrot of the the quarterly cash and the stick of adult pressures – from both home and chapel – kept them at it. But they got satisfaction out of it as well.

As each boy reached the stage of singing solos Mum's attendance would become more regular again. I sensed – and shared – her pride in them when they appeared from the vestry and passed so close to us, deliberately positioned as we were at the end nearest the aisle of a pew near the front. Their hands neatly folded across their short white surplices, faces polished, they were transformed from their normal everyday scruffiness. All of them had their hair smarmed down and gleaming on each side of perfect partings – Wally dark and rosy-cheeked, Joe golden-fair, Pete always with his eyes cast down and Ken with his rolling upwards.

Side by side in the congregation Mum and I handled our prayer books, sang the hymns and psalms, made the responses, dipped our heads and sank on our knees with the confident familiarity born of long practice. It was a joy to me to hear Mum's warbles and trills, to share her pride in me beside her, and even more in Wally or Joe when they sang a solo in their pure, high voices.

After the service was over, we filed out slowly with the rest of the congregation, Mum having a quiet word on the way with those amongst the congregation with whom she was on friendly terms. There was, at this point, no need to hurry because the boys had to get out of their gowns before they could join us outside the porch, under the limes growing each side of the small gravel path leading into Lampmead Road. Before we could cover these few yards between the porch and the wrought iron gate Mum had to greet and shake hands with the curate with a suitably humbled demeanour. It was once we had passed this point that the serenity inspired by the service had a habit of evaporating rapidly. Mum would have preferred it if we could have become actually invisible at this point. As we could not, we had to do our best to spirit ourselves away as inconspicuously as possible.

The problem for Mum was that having gone to the trouble, as she saw it, of dressing up to go out she felt she needed more than an hour's service to make the effort worthwhile. For this reason she almost invariably planned to join Dad at the pub or the club, going straight there from the church.

It was ridiculous, but we all assumed that the curate – or, even worse, the rector when he occasionally honoured us with a visit – would know where she was off to if he caught sight of her turning up the road in the opposite direction from home. And maybe he did, although I very much doubt whether he had such a sharp awareness of who we were, let alone what we were up to, as we presumed he had. In any case, as many people had relatives all over Lee and going for Sunday evening walks was quite a common practice there is no reason why he should have judged correctly where we were off to. It all came from Mum. Brought up, as she had been, in a religious and inflexibly teetotal home, she was deeply imbued with the notion that drink was not favoured by God or the godly. To her, going straight from chapel to pub was to go from the righteous to the sinful. By a mixture of her instructions to us on how we were to behave and our sense of her guilt, we absorbed her unease.

This did not prevent me and, I suppose the boys too, from longing to go with her, and each time the anxiety arose whether or not we were to be allowed to. If she had arranged to meet Dad up the pub there was no question but that we children had to go home. The licensing laws prevented us going inside the pub and Dad's own law forbade us to stay outside. If she was going to join Dad at the club it depended partly on her mood and, more often than not, how Dad was fixed financially that week. I never knew what swung the decision either way. It was not simply the money, for sometimes she would say, 'You can come, but you're not to ask for anything. We're short this week.' She would never say in advance whether or not we could go. It was always at the last minute that the decision was made (or so it seemed to us). Pete and Ken were not involved in this recurrent drama. Grandad did not belong to the club and never went to it, and in any case Gran always expected her boys back home straight after the service to make sure no harm came to their best Sunday clothes.

For us upstairs the visits to the Lee Working Men's Club gradually replaced the Sunday night booze-ups in Gran's front room. After Uncle Bert died we still had Harold, one of Gran's twins, to play for us. He could not play as well but he could 'vamp' a tune (one of those adult words I never understood and no one explained). But even so, gradually on some Sunday nights as well as Saturdays, Mum began to go off up the pub or the club to join Dad. When we were left behind we hated it. We were not alone in the house but to cause Gran to come upstairs would, we knew, mean trouble with Mum because she would have to face not only Gran's complaints about us but her implied criticism of Mum for having gone out. On a Sunday night if there was something going on in the front room it was harder still. Gran was less likely to hear us quarrelling and scuffling about upstairs, but we could hear the noise of the fun we were missing. In Mum and Dad's absence we were not allowed to join the adults downstairs, and we envied Pete and Ken who were.

Unlike Mum, I had no strong feelings that drink was sinful, rather a very strong feeling that being with adults in party spirits was good. From an early age, too, I saw being allowed to take part in the fun as a reward for goodness. It was a short step from this to believing that a bit of godliness might sway the balance on a Sunday night as to whether or not I would be able to go to the club.

At Boone's Chapel, eyes tightly shut to ensure concentration, I would send up my prayer: 'Please God, let her take me up the club tonight.' I cannot say I ever had much proof of God's success in interceding on my behalf, but I was always hopeful. In fact, Wally was more often allowed to go than I was. It was not just that he was the eldest (and the one who most clearly earned this reward by helping Mum in all kinds of ways). Incomprehensibly, to me, Mum regarded him as more of a companion to her – and less of a worry. I never had the sense, as Wally did, to be content to remain an observer, I was always out to prove my worth by joining in. More often than not my attempts to take part in the gossiping led to a sharp response from Mum. 'You be quiet. You know nothing about it,' she would say to me, and then to her friends, in exasperated tones, 'You can't say a thing without her poking her nose in.' To me the risk of rebuffs was a small price to pay for the joys of Sunday evenings up the club.

The club was – and still is – close by Lee Green on the way up the hill to Blackheath. A large detached house, built as a private residence in 1850, it is set well back from the road and has a large garden behind it. To one side is an extension which was clearly originally servants' quarters. On the other side another extension, probably built as a coach house, had been converted into a hall after it became the Lee Working Men's Club in 1907. It was to the hall, during winter (or wet weather in summer), that the wives and children went at weekends. The bar and the games room, where darts, billiards or cards could be enjoyed, were strictly for the men. (There was a separate women's room, as well as the hall, where drinks bought at the bar by husbands were brought in to the wives from time to time.)

On Saturday nights there was usually a concert where semi-professional comedians, dancers, singers and conjurers did their turns on the small stage. On Sundays the hall was cleared for dancing with seats and tables pushed against the walls.

For most of the time, during the 'shows' or the dancing, the menfolk were seen only occasionally in the hall. They came in from time to time to bring wives, friends' wives and the children more drinks. But it was only late in the evening, when they had reached the stage of beery good humour, that husbands began to join their wives in the dancing. Few of the men danced well, and those who did (and spent more time dancing than drinking) were, in my memory at least, smaller than the average, more neatly dressed and with few, if any children. Whereas such men danced frequently with their wives, Mum and her friends danced mostly with each other or – towering head and shoulders above them – with their own children. But with luck, even if only for the last waltz, the women would eventually have the pleasure of propelling their befuddled menfolk round the floor.

It was at the club that Mum taught Wally and I how to waltz and how to dance the Valeta. This is how it was for most children, but one boy, a friend of Wally's, had had real dancing lessons; he manoeuvred his mother round the floor with a stiff perfection that was much admired. He looked even more dashing, in his smart Sunday suit and with fair, short hair, well-greased down, when he danced with a girl of around his own age who, unlike his mother, was about his own height. I longed for the day to come when he would ask me to dance (I believe I prayed for this too at Boone's Chapel). He was often urged by his relatives to give me a try, but he never condescended to do so.

In the summer months the dances and concerts took place in the garden, which had a large central lawn and was edged by flower-beds. There were no doubt abundant herbaceous borders when the house was a private residence but these had become bare and neg-lected. Still, on a fine summer's evening when the tables and chairs were set out on the large lawn under a bright sky it was pleasant enough. Even more so on bank holidays when amusements, com-petitions and races organized specially for the children created an atmosphere much like that at the fair on Blackheath.

A long shed by the side entry of the house was used as an open-air bar, where crates and crates of beer and mineral waters were stacked. Alongside this ramshackle bar were two stalls run by club members who had been given the franchise to sell snacks. From Charlie's we could buy cheese sandwiches, or hot saveloys whose taut shiny red skins broke with a snap as our teeth bit into them. They had a soggy pink filling which tasted mainly of bread. Adults helped themselves to liberal dollops of the fierce, yellow mustard from the large jar on the counter. I liked the colour of the yellow against the pink but knew from experience that the mustard was much hotter than the saveloy.

At the second stall Harry Drury sold his home-made horse-radish, pickled onions and jellied eels. Red-faced and jovial, he was well liked although he was not a 'local' man, living as he did a mile away. The horseradish he used was harvested from a railway bank close to his house. He had a great brood of children, one of whom became a friend of mine for a brief while. I once went to call for her at their house (which has long since been demolished to make way for the parking behind the shopping centre at Lewi-sham). One of a small terrace built in yellow brick, it was probably older than our houses at Lee and had a cottagey atmosphere which made me think of Blunham. The front door was left open to enable the numerous children and neighbours to come and go freely. Mrs Drury, a plump, placid woman, seemed entirely untroubled by either her chaotic and crowded surroundings, or by the smell of horseradish. The house was more than suffused with this smell, it was impregnated to such a degree that it made one's eyes water and tingle. Harry's own eyes were perpetually weeping and red-rimmed and yet his children all had bright, clear blue eyes and fine, pale complexions.

Dad was fond of Harry because he was always ready to provide a loan in hard times, and also to give us a jar of horseradish or pickles to help us out. Even so, he was not considered to be quite up to our own social standing. He had too many children and he lived in Lewisham – in a poor part of it at that – so he was judged to be 'a bit rough and ready, but all right'.

When we were up the club there was always an ebb and flow about us of people familiar to us. Unlike the ties with our family, those at the club were often transitory. I suspect that this instability of relationships between some members was closely linked to a complex pattern of borrowing and lending – and promises made and broken over repayments. Unaware of these undercurrents, we children drifted easily – and indeed were encouraged by the adults – into calling any non-relatives who came into our circle for a week or two 'uncle' or 'auntie'. It seemed natural enough as temporarily they had become part of the general family of adult life which surrounded us. When one 'uncle' and 'aunt' moved out of the circle, there were always others to move in; always someone to tease or pet us, to buy us crisps, saveloys or lemonade. Like satellites, they encircled what was for us the real centre, the permanent unchangeable figures of Mum and Dad.

Dad

Jack, who had won a scholarship to the direct-grant school of St Dunstan's College, was not the only one of Dad's brothers to do well at school. For some reason, however – most likely expense – Grandad did not allow all his sons to take up the educational opportunities offered them and Uncle Bert, for one, was bitter about this in adult life. Dad, however, was 'no scholar'. He had a hard time at the church school a street or two away round the corner, where caning was commonplace and a hard crack across the knuckles with a ruler inevitable for any bad spelling or writing. Dad, according to his own account, 'could do anything with figures but was no good at writing'. At eleven he left school and was put to work at a local garage with the prospect of becoming an apprentice mechanic. In fact he never became an apprentice, but as a result of his experience was drafted into the Royal Engineers when his time came for war service.

Of all Gran's nine boys, Alec, my father, was her favourite. When small he had been somewhat delicate. This, coupled with his angelic fairness of hair and skin, and his vivid blue eyes, perhaps compensated Gran a little for the daughter she had lost and never replaced. A hint of an almost feminine delicacy of movement and a marked personal fastidiousness remained with this in other ways rough man throughout his life. Strangely, when he was drunk (or at any rate not sober) this delicacy of movement became more noticeable, but the fastidiousness was displaced by a coarseness of conduct which was sometimes revolting.

100

When Dad, invalided home from Egypt, met Mum at Ladywell he was still fair-haired and fine-skinned, but then he was not much more than a boy, still in his early twenties. By the time my memories of him begin, his thick, slightly wavy hair had darkened to a nondescript brown; his complexion was roughened from constant exposure to the weathers and his forearms and legs were covered in a forest of brown, soft hair. Tall, bony-kneed and long-thighed, he had through hard manual work developed a taut strength in the basically slender frame. After tea, when he still sat at the table, relaxed and good-humoured and with his shirt-sleeves rolled up to the elbow, he would sometimes amuse me by flexing the muscles in his forearms as I touched them. This movement, like some small animal crawling under his skin, never failed to make me squeal with a mixture of excitement and horror.

Morning and evening he stripped off his shirt and washed in cold water at the sink in the scullery. Winter and summer, day and night, he wore a round-necked, sleeved vest so that there was not a very large area of him exposed for these ablutions. But he made up for this in the thoroughness with which he lathered and splashed his arms, neck and face. Leaning almost into the bowl of cold water, he would slosh handfuls of water onto himself again and again, making loud blowing noises to keep the water out of his nose and mouth. We lived so close and intimately in the little space upstairs, but I never saw Dad in the bath, or without his vest and trousers (or his pyjamas) though I often saw his long sinewy feet and hairy calves when he soaked them in a bowl in the kitchen to soften his corns before cutting them about with a cut-throat razor.

Once, when with unusual carelessness he was tucking in a clean shirt Mum had just ironed for him, his trousers dropped and I caught a glimpse of his 'private parts' through the gap in his long woollen underpants. To me, this glimpse of reddish flesh and dark hairiness was startling; what I saw in no way resembled the soft exposed whiteness I knew from the games under the bushes with my brothers and cousins. Linking this up with what I had seen of his hairy arms and legs, I assumed from then on that Dad's entire body was covered in hair and a mesh of crawling muscles. It was many years later when I saw his uncovered body for the first time. The day before he died in hospital of lung cancer, when he was past protesting, the nurses removed his vest. His lily-white chest was hairless, and thin as a boy's.

Partly because of Mum's threats, we early became fearful of incurring Dad's displeasure. I am told that once when I was troublesome on my way home from shopping at Lewisham Dad took me up a side-way and slapped my bum hard. I have no memory of this, and he never hit me again, or my brothers at all. Mum sometimes said he was afraid, if he ever did hit us, that he would be in such a rage he would kill us. On rare occasions he would raise an arm at us, and threaten to strike. This was frightening enough to silence us instantly. To me he seemed so powerful that I almost believed that, like God, he too had the power and the right literally to strike us dead if he chose to. Most of the time he needed only to speak sharply or to glare at us with his blue eyes flashing in anger. His anger was never simulated, and we knew it. When we heard Dad and Mum quarrelling in the night our world rocked round us; Dad's voice cracked like thunder and we knew from experience there was lightning in his eyes.

Normally Dad did not raise his voice at us. In fact, he spoke both quietly and briefly on all occasions except when he had 'been on the beer'. He had an inviolable rule of never repeating anything he said to us. He felt it showed lack of respect in a child not to pay attention to him sufficiently to hear what he said first time. We suffered from this because, like all children, our minds were for ever on 'something else' – a book, a game, an argument between ourselves. However much we asked him, even begged him, to repeat what he had said (busily giving our excuses for not having heard him the first time), he would not do so. Exasperatingly, the most he would say was 'You heard me the first time,' or 'If you wanted to hear, you should have listened.' At other times he would just shut his thin lips even tighter, so that they completely disappeared, and remain silent. Worst of all, he had a useful knack of implying by his expression that we had missed hearing something to our advantage – like 'Do you want a piece of chocolate?' – whereas he had probably only said something we didn't want to hear like 'Get my slippers'!

When he started work at the age of eleven Dad began to smoke. Drinking followed not long afterwards. Smoking and drinking became the main pleasures of his life. His need for both added to our material difficulties, yet looking back it is hard to see how such a man at such a time could have gone on at all without their help. That tense frame, those tight lips, those long, ascetic features which made him look like a younger brother of Bertrand Russell, concealed and protected in a harsh world – the only one he knew for most of his life – a sensitive man of sharp intelligence and painful pride.

Dad's years in Egypt made a great impression on him. What he saw there of a pre-Christian civilization increased his doubts over the religion he had been exposed to at school and church. He sent us children to Sunday school, took it for granted his sons should be choirboys as he himself had been, and on rare occasions could be dragged along by Mum to evensong at Boone's Chapel, at the end of our road, or the parish church of St Margaret's at Blackheath. He never, in other words, openly flouted or mocked the religion he had been brought up in. For many years only Mum knew that in his view Christianity made no more sense for the ordinary working man than some of the more primitive religions he had noted on his travels.

After their marriage, when work was already difficult to find, Dad had wanted to return to Egypt as a policeman. Mum was against this, and it was then that Dad turned to the building trade. At first he travelled to London, working with big firms and earning a lot of overtime money in good months. By observation and then trial and error, he grasped the rudiments of the various crafts, like plastering, painting, bricklaying and plumbing. His schooldays had provided him with sufficient expertise at carpentry. He began to help an old school friend of his who had got to the local grammar school and later trained to be a surveyor. This friend, Cyril Parker, lived in a semi-detached house in Lenham Road, which was the second of the two roads branching off at right angles from ours, and was a bit more classy. Cyril had his own surveyor's business, but he also carried on the small building firm that had been his father's. At times when he was too busy Dad worked for him on the understanding that Cyril would teach him what he could to improve his skills.

Once he had begun to work locally Dad realized how much he preferred to save the fares and the travelling time, but most of all the time wasted hanging about for buses or trams. Even when Cyril did not need him, from then on he looked for work locally. Locally, mind you, for him meant within a walking distance of up to three miles or, for the rare and exceptionally attractive job, a short tram or bus ride to places like New Cross or Woolwich. He began to dream of becoming 'his own master' with a small firm, like Cyril's. The depression years made this dream even more attractive when in the bad, winter months he walked for miles around seeking work at all the places he knew of.

Sometimes he was offered work at below the accepted hourly rate. Mum felt aggrieved if he told her of such offers he had refused. In her view anything was better than nothing. To Dad, cut-rates were an insult: he would rather starve – and have us starve too – than tolerate them. For him, it was not a question of 'blacklegging' or undermining workers' solidarity. He was no trade unionist. He simply considered that he earned, and deserved, the full rate for the job. His pride would not allow him to accept any less. He loathed, of course, the indignity of 'signing on' at the Labour Exchange. On one exceptional occasion when he was out of benefit he applied for help from 'Public Assistance' and came home so distressed that even Mum preferred we should all starve, rather than inflict such agony on him again. Somehow we always managed to survive: by owing Grandad the rent for months on end, letting insurances go, buying food on 'tick', borrowing from the loan club, the publican and any other better-placed 'friends'.

Gran would never refuse a request from Dad for half-a-crown 'to keep him in fags'. And in desperate moments even Dad would pass on the half-a-crown to Mum to buy food, and exist miserably fag-less.

It was an exciting day when Dad put up his board on the wall to the left of the front door. Another old school friend, a signwriter by trade, had 'made a nice job' of the sign. 'A. G. Noble', it read, 'Builder and Decorator'. Jordan had agreed to let Dad fix studs on the long side wall of her alley on which to hang his ladders. Cyril agreed to loan him a builder's handcart whenever he needed it, and any other larger items of equipment requiring storage space he had not got. At last he was his own master. He never again had to join the long, drab queues at the 'Labour'. But times were not much better for us. He had no capital to fall back on so that slack periods were as disastrous as before.

And now, as a self-employed man, he was no longer eligible for unemployment benefit, short-term and inadequate as it was. In bad times he spent just as much time walking about the district looking for work. The difference was that he was now calling on his own 'customers', trying to persuade them to have the house re-painted a bit earlier than they had intended, or perhaps just enquiring how some earlier work had turned out – in the hope that his appearance might suggest some other job that needed doing.

Such an energetic man as Dad could only enjoy sitting back in his chair, reading his paper or listening to the wireless, at the end of the day, when it had been justified by a 'good day's' work. To find him at home in the middle of the day with no work behind him, was a warning to us that, frustrated by inactivity, he was likely to be irritable. A cautiously friendly 'Hello Dad' might qualify for a jerk of the leonine head, or the slightest acknowledgment by a lift of the short bushy eyebrows as he sat, brooding and silent, trying to make his home-made fag last as long as he could.

It was a sign of hard times when Dad was rolling his own fags. The only good thing about it was that we enjoyed making them for him. He kept two tins on his side of the mantelpiece, one for tobacco ready for rolling, the other for the cigarette papers and the 'roller', which made up the fags, and the 'dog ends' of fags already smoked. When a suitable pile of ends had collected, the first job was to remove the chewed and discoloured paper round the half-inch stub and sift and pull this apart before adding it to the 'new' tobacco in the other tin. Cigarettes in the roller had to be carefully prepared so that the tobacco lay smoothly and evenly distributed along the length of the roller. They had to be not too thick (this used up too much tobacco), or too tight (this made them hard to smoke), or too loose (they would burn up too quickly).

When money was not so tight, Dad preferred to smoke Weights or Woodbines. During the week he would often be left with only just enough money in his pocket to 'see him through the week' for his fags and his midday pint of beer. These, with at most a sandwich, got him through even the hardest day's work. He could seldom be persuaded to eat a cooked breakfast. In general he ate moderately for such an active man. He enjoyed, and in Mum's view needed, protein in the form of chops, steaks, the much favoured smoked haddock, herrings and shellfish. Potatoes and vegetables he invariably, and to Mum's constant irritation, 'picked at', eating only one or two mouthfuls before putting them aside. He rarely ate puddings, although if they were disguised by a sufficiently thick covering of custard he could sometimes be tempted. Always anxious to 'keep up his strength', Mum encouraged his finicky ways by her continual concern over his food. She would hover round, or sit in her chair looking at him anxiously from her wide-open brown eyes to see how he was going to react to the first mouthful. If he declared the meat to be tough, or the herrings not fresh, she was off in a whirl of words trying to persuade him it couldn't or shouldn't be so. She couldn't bear either the waste of the food, or that he had not had enough to eat. But however much she urged and persuaded, like a petulant child he would take at most just one more reluctant mouthful, grimace, turn aside from the offending plate, then brusquely demand the next course, or the cup of tea which always rounded off the meal.

Like Grandad, Dad was an early riser. In the week, Mum got up first to make him tea, but he was often the one who woke her. He was also punctual to an obsessive degree. Weekend visits to the pub were timed to the minute. It was not good form to arrive before the doors were open and have to hang about outside, but he planned to arrive virtually as the door unlocked. Similarly it was not enough to arrive on time for work: he made a habit of being there a good ten minutes earlier. Invariably in good time, yet always in fear of being late, he hurried out of the house each weekday morning with an air of urgency. One morning after he had gone Mum noticed that he had left his cigarettes on the table. 'Quick,' she cried out, handing me the Weights, 'run after your Dad. He's gone through the park – catch him.' She probably knew he had not enough money on him to buy another packet that morning – and she certainly knew that his day would be a misery without a smoke.

I ran as fast as I could along uphill Aislibie Road, round the corner into Old Road, and by this time I was gasping for breath. When I reached the park gates I could see him passing the lavatories and about to turn by the great elm tree. By then, a painful stitch prevented me calling to him. I could not run on and also cry out. It was always hard work – a process of half-running – to keep up with him even when out walking. Now, in a hurry, his long legs were scissoring back and forwards at a dizzy pace. I felt I was in a dream, as I forced myself to run on and on, each step an agony. I drew closer, I tried to call but only a whispered 'Dad' came out, which he could not have heard. More likely the sound of my running caught his ear. He turned round and stopped. Gasping for breath, I managed to gulp out, 'Your fags, Dad; you forgot your fags.' 'Thanks mate' – he took them and walked on.

As I stood there trying to get my breath back and looking after him, he turned round again and came back towards me. With a rare gesture of concern, he put his hand on my head. The thickened fingers which looked too big and clumsy for his stringy yet graceful frame, pushed the hair off my prickling hot face. He even stooped

a little to look more closely at me as he asked, 'You all right, girl?'
At that perfect moment my eyes brimmed with tears as I nodded
silently and smiled painfully.

The same energy which made him race along creating a wind to
set his trousers flapping like rudders above the heels of his shoes,
also helped to keep him occupied even when paid work was impossible to find. The bath and geyser were early improvements upstairs.
Later, he ripped out the kitchen range which required so much
hard work and elbow grease to keep its shining pewter-like glow.
A little open basket-style grate and an oak overmantel replaced it.
This meant we no longer had 'Granny Mann' style rice puddings
cooked in the slowness of the old range-oven, but we were only too
pleased to forgo such advantages for the pleasure of making our
'kitchen' less kitcheny. Dad planned his improvements and decora-
tions carefully. Having decided what was needed, he 'kept his
eyes open' for the desired new equipment. Sooner or later in his
interminable walking about the district he would see what he
wanted, possibly cast aside on a building lot, or in a second-hand
shop, or even on one of his own jobs. If it was reasonable to do so,
he 'knocked it off', as often as not with the connivance of his mates
or fellow-workers on other sites. If he had to buy, he was patient
enough to be prepared to wait if, on a first enquiry, 'the price was
not right'.

In the same way, 'new' furniture came in to displace things like
the old Edwardian sofa on which I had first seen Joey. A big,
upholstered armchair on one side of the fire came for Dad, and a
wooden-framed armchair with an adjustable back for Mum. One
day half a dozen 'dining-room chairs' turned up and were with
some difficulty crammed into the room. The plywood with which
Dad covered the top of the old kitchen table had to be bought new,
but the stains and varnish with which Dad simulated a solid,
polished 'modern' table were no doubt 'picked up' on his jobs.
Paper for the kitchen walls, paint, distemper, trestles and buckets
and so on were 'knocked off' or 'borrowed' from somewhere as
Dad came to need them.

However long the weeks off work dragged on, Dad did not expect to be asked to help with household chores. Not even when Mum, in desperation and against his wishes, took on a morning charring job for the gentle Misses Peasgood in Lenham Road. Dad was only prepared to do jobs which were appropriate for men. He acquired a pair of hairdresser's scissors – and clippers too – so that he could cut our hair. And his small iron last, with prongs to fit three sizes of shoes, was brought up from the shed downstairs almost weekly. For this work he would go off and buy a square of new leather, on which he pencil-marked the shape of the soles or heels to be replaced, laboriously cut them out with a tough knife, then soaked them for hours until the water had turned yellow and the leather had become pliable, before beginning the job of ripping off the old soles from our shoes and tacking on the new. Sometimes the tacks he had to use were not quite the most suitable, or his skill not quite that of the craftsman shoemaker. At school, or out and about one day, we would find a nail had worked up through the sole into the ball or toe of a foot. It made every step a misery, as the nail re-entered the punctured flesh.

Back at home, Dad would get out his last again and knock the tack out or flatten the sharp tip causing the trouble against the inner sole. Horrible crescents of steel tapped on the tips of toes and heels to make the leather last longer, were another disadvantage to put up with. They made the shoes seem not only heavy but bumpy and unlevel at first. And as they struck the pavement the metal tips made a noise, and sometimes even sparks, that seemed all right for boys, but not at all appropriately 'light-footed' for a girl. 'Only put one on Dad, just one, only one, for me,' I begged. Mum felt the same as I did, and eventually Dad began to buy for us only very small ones which had names like 'Fairy Tips' or 'Quiet Imps'.

One gain to us when Dad was out of work was that he had to stay at home more in the evenings. We had the wireless to listen to, and, in desperation, Dad would occasionally get a book to read to pass the time after he had read the paper from cover to cover. Best

of all, he – or we – would suggest a game of snakes and ladders,
ludo, dominoes or cards. As soon as we were big enough to play
with any kind of sense, Dad preferred the card games. When he
was 'well-breeched', playing at cards for money was the only form
of gambling which held any interest for him. Mum hated it when
the passion temporarily seized him and he would get into a 'card
school' which would, after pub hours, move on to someone's home
to continue play with much bigger stakes all afternoon or late into
the night. Sometimes on a Saturday afternoon the 'school' came
back to play in Gran's front room. I would be called on to take
down tea or sandwiches from time to time. Angrily Mum prepared
them and I took them down – delighted to get the threepences or
sixpences the men showered on me. On these occasions Mum knew
that if his luck was out, Dad might end up so 'skint' that he would
have to ask her for money back from the housekeeping to keep him
in beer and fags the rest of the week. It could also happen the other
way round, when a 'school' began before Dad had come home to
give Mum her money, so that most of the housekeeping money
would be lost as well. Horse-racing or 'the dogs' had no attraction
for Dad, he considered them 'mug's games' because they seemed to
him to demand no skill – and therefore allowed no control over
what happened. With cards, he had to admit, luck could be a
decisive factor but skill played an important part too.

There is no doubt that Dad's skill at cards was of a high order.
One of the things that made cards at home such fun was Dad's –
to me – magic powers at card games. For years I was baffled how
he apparently knew the cards that everyone else held in their
hands, as well as any left on the table. Wally would angrily accuse
him of cheating as Dad looked across and asked, 'How about
putting down that ace of spades you've got there?', yet at the same
time Wally knew this knowledge could not have been gained unfairly. Cheating was against the code. The code could, of course,
be twisted a bit for 'babies' – or girls – and in fact for me it
frequently was. By sitting next to Dad I made sure of getting his
advice, which I certainly needed. Unlike him, I was incapable of

concentrating enough to remember the cards in my own hand, let alone what lay elsewhere on the table. With Dad's help, however, when the halfpennies were collected up and paid out, I was more likely to be 'up' than 'down', to the disgust of my brothers. The familiar tall figure whose bony knees pressed large shiny discs onto his trouser legs as he sat reading his paper, and the silent, rather sombre man who whisked by me at play with a brief, quizzical smile was not the same person we came to know would appear after an hour or three 'up the pub'. All the dignity of manner which his normally withdrawn and reserved personality imposed on him, seemed to vanish once he 'got on the booze'. His distant reticence, which kept us children always a little in awe of him, was replaced by a smart good humour and a kind of sharp repartee which could suddenly turn sour. His reddened nose, two high spots of crimson on his cheeks, and a silly grin gave his face a comic's look which put us on our guard. 'He'll be all ha-ha-ha and hee-hee-hee when he comes in,' Mum would say bitterly, then go on to warn us once again not to rely on his temper and, at all costs, to avoid any indication of dismay or disgust. Influenced by Mum, our disgust became harder to conceal as we grew older and under-stood more clearly the price Mum had to pay for Dad's 'boozing'. When the inevitable quarrels began, and Dad spat out his words, swearing at Mum with increasing violence and filth, and she in turn shrilled and swore back, our love for him seemed to be swamped by waves of misery and hate. Mum often appeared to take a kind of martyred satisfaction in drawing his revolting behaviour to our notice. How he had sloshed his beery piss as much over the floor as in the bucket; how his loud and smelly wet farts had made shit-marks on his pyjamas or, even worse, the sheets.

Next morning, however it had been the night before, Dad would be once again his silent, preoccupied, everyday self. He might, if asked, confess to feeling 'a bit rough', his manner to Mum if she was still unfriendly might be brusque, but to us he was if anything a little more friendly, a little less distant than usual. If it was a Sunday morning, which was most likely, since heavy drinking for him was almost entirely a weekend or holiday indulgence, he went off downstairs early to have his half-hour's piano practice in Gran's front room before going to see her for the ritual Sunday morning gathering in her kitchen. He did not play well, but he played from music, and he was inordinately proud of this. From time to time he bought a new sheet of music for some new and popular tune and practised hard on these Sunday mornings to master it.

Sometimes he succeeded in using his playing to woo Mum back to him again after a Saturday-night quarrel. At the piano his odd, almost feminine, delicacy came out most clearly. His mouth would be pursed up in a tight, short line as he concentrated hard on reading the music. His hands, the thick fingers stiff from their constant exposure to the elements and all kinds of abrasive paints and plasters, battled to touch the keys lightly and precisely, in the way his music teacher long ago had instructed him. Inside the house or out of it, active or at rest in bed or chair, soberly silent or raffishly waggish, his quixotic personality ruled our lives. 'Your father,' my mother told us frequently, her baffled resignation tinged with admiration, 'your father is a very peculiar man.'

12

School

On the day after my third birthday I was taken to join my brother at the LCC kindergarten school on the 'other side' of the park. Each afternoon during the year in which Wally had been going to the kindergarten, Mum had taken Joey and me to meet him at the end of the afternoon session. I was only too eager to join him at school, and settled down immediately to the long walk through the park, and down the strange roads on the other side to Manor Lane School. In the mornings, a big girl from up the road took us, shepherded us home again at lunch-time and called for us to go back again after lunch. It was a long journey – four times a day – for small children, but broken as it was by the walk through the park it was mostly only on the coldest and greyest of wintry days that it seemed a hardship. In summer, Mum would bring a picnic tea for us to eat on the green slope of the park on the way home. In the autumn there was the joy of collecting acorns or bunches of plane tree leaves with their pretty patterns and colours, or wading and kicking through the piles of leaves collecting in the gutters. In winter there was the magic of looking up into the tall evergreen trees sheltering the pair of sleepy owls, or of feeding stale bread to the hungry ducks swimming forlornly in their small pool of water where the keepers had broken the ice on the pond. And then as the days began to brighten again there was the daily search under the elm for the sight of the first crocus bud, certain herald of the carpet of orange, white and mauve to follow, and of the daffodils bunched beneath the oak trees on the other side.

The kindergarten at Manor Lane School was a separate build-ing of two rooms, but sharing the same gateway and playground as the Infants. Miss Hodges was our teacher when I arrived. She had tobacco-brown hair, piled up on her head in an Edwardian frizzy nest. She was tall and long-featured. Beyond the entrance, where we hung our coats and changed our shoes, was a large room with plain wooden nursery tables and small chairs set out in lines, like desks in any classroom, facing the dais on which Miss Hodges' table was set. In the mornings we sat at our tables, cutting out and making paper toys, drawing patterns in dry sand in small trays, fitting coloured shapes into cut-out wooden blocks, singing count-ing rhymes and endlessly reciting the alphabet. It was a long time before I understood what the mysterious 'Ella-mena-pee-q' had to do with letters, but I loved everything we did. Back home in the evenings I stood on the seat of Dad's armchair performing over and over again what we had learnt from Miss Hodges, until Mum could stand no more and told me to stop.

In the afternoons, on our return from lunch, we turned our tables upside down so that their legs pointed upwards, and lay down on these 'beds' for our rest. For the remainder of the after-noon session we moved through into the second room for more active games and pursuits. This room was empty except for the chairs round the walls, a maypole with coloured ribbons in the centre, and a pony-sized dappled-grey rocking-horse by the door. At playtime, we clustered under the shelter opposite the kinder-garten door, and keeping away from the 'bigger' children stayed like shy ducklings as close as we could to our building. On fine summer days Miss Hodges marshalled us into a crocodile, issued us each a bucket and small wooden spade and walked us down beyond the shelter, across a tangled patch of land looking like a neglected allotment, to a sand-pit, where she sat knitting while we played.

Eighteen months later, school and Miss Hodges were as much part of life as Mum and home. It was the end of the Easter holi-days and I was delighted at the prospect of returning to tell this

austere but lovable teacher all that I had been doing while away
from her. I did not ask why, but on this morning Mum came with
us, helping to carry the enormous bunch of lilac she had filched
under Grandad's disapproving eye from the mauve-massed bushes
in the garden. Once at the school, I was not allowed to go inside
the familiar building but had to wait with Mum and some other
children and parents in the shelter. Then, heading a familiar crocodile of children, Miss Hodges emerged, leading her little tribe out
of the kindergarten and across to the infants' building. 'Quick,'
said Mum, grabbing one hand and pushing the bunch of lilac into
the other, 'quick. Catch Miss Hodges before she's gone!' Suddenly,
I knew what was happening. They were all going up to the Infants'
school, whereas I for some incomprehensible reason was to be left
behind. Miss Hodges, attracted by Mum calling her name, told her
children to halt at the door and came to greet us. 'Give Miss
Hodges her flowers,' Mum urged. 'No!' I said, clutching them
tight, tears falling fast. 'No. I won't!' Miss Hodges leaned down
and explained that I would join her again later, but for now I had
to stay in the kindergarten a bit longer. To me her reasons carried
no conviction. I recognized only her betrayal and my misery, and
only by force could Mum remove the bunch of lilac from my determined grasp to give it herself to Miss Hodges.

When, some months later, I did 'go up' to the Infants I liked it –
and Miss Hodges with whom I was reunited – almost as much,
although it was hard no longer to have afternoons in the sand-pit
or rides on 'Dobbin'. The Infants' school was larger than the
kindergarten, with six or seven classrooms round a hall covered by
a glass roof. The high-spot of the year was Christmas-time. Soon
after it began to get about amongst us that 'Christmas is only eight
weeks away', going to school in the darkening mornings held its
own pleasure of anticipation. Every morning we rushed into the
playground to a corner of the Infants' school building where a
brick buttress jutted out from the main wall. In this corner we
knew, one day, 'the tree' would arrive. Seven or eight feet tall,
trussed with ropes, one morning it would be leaning there waiting

for us. After it had been carried inside, untied and set up in the middle of the hall, each class was allotted an afternoon to work on its decoration. Miss Hodges' usual contribution was to bring a large tin of dolly mixture sweets, which with her class's help were put into tiny net bags and tied with loops of coloured twine. On our afternoon of 'decoration', Miss Hodges climbed up the ladder by the tree, and a few picked pupils handed up the sweets to be hung on the branches. I found it an easy matter to slip a bag up my knicker leg. Dawdling a safe distance behind Mum, I fished them out to eat, guiltily and surreptitiously – but none the less enjoyably – on our way home through the park.

Joey, Mum's 'baby', was never sent to the kindergarten. He was, on the contrary, kept at home with Mum until the very latest 'compulsory' date for beginning school. Even then Mum, loath perhaps to have her baby further away than he need be, enrolled him at the nearby church school which Dad and his brothers had attended, and where Gran had already sent cousins Peter and Ken. When first Wally, then I, reached the age to go up to the Junior school, Mum wanted to transfer us to Northbrook to join the others. When my turn came, Mum had to see the headmistress in the hall after school. I hung around nearby. Since I had to go to a 'new' school anyway – the Juniors at Manor Lane School had its own entrance and playground – I did not mind the idea of moving to the Church school instead.

The headmistress, however, was far less prepared for me to go. I pricked up my ears as I heard her arguing with Mum, and the phrase 'we shall have to chain her to the railings' caught my attention. Mum was having an uncomfortable few minutes, for as it became clear she was determined to move me, the headmistress's voice (which had begun in almost humorous tones) became less amused. It seemed that Mum was plucking the fruit that Manor Lane School, if it had not planted, had at least nourished successfully. 'You are taking away one of our brightest stars,' the headmistress ended accusingly. Her felicitous turn of phrase opened my eyes. I had always enjoyed the praise for good work given me by

Miss Hodges. I strove hard to please her by getting good marks for writing or sums, or indeed in any way I could. It was only at that moment that I became aware I was not merely a 'good' girl trying hard to please.

Northbrook School was a smaller school than Manor Lane School. Infants and junior girls, although in separate single-storey buildings, shared the same playground. The boys' building – juniors and seniors combined – adjoined the girls', but it had its own entrance and playground. The headmaster of the boys' was the same man as when Dad was a boy. He was now able to clump another generation of Noble boys over the knuckles with his long ruler whenever he took a lesson and found their spelling at fault. He was no monster, no sadist avid for punishment, just a teacher of the 'old school' trying to do his best for his pupils. Old boys, like Dad, were very fond of him, and always pleased to have a word with him when their paths crossed on their travels about Lee.

Miss Hemsley, the headmistress of the junior girls, was a small, plain-faced woman with dark hair worn in a loose, low bun. She was precise and cool in manner, rather than strict or severe, though once she did slap my forearm with a fierce deliberation when she caught me inking in all the circular bits to the numbers in my arithmetic book.

The church school belonged to our parish and was our nearest school. I already knew some of the girls well – my old friend Beaty Couldrey, for example. Others I knew by sight. The Rector, who often visited the school, I also knew by sight from Sunday school and church attendance. It was therefore easy for me to settle down in the new school, but I remember a 'big' girl's disbelief and near-indignation in the playground soon after I began. She had heard I was 'new' and came across to question this because, in her view, I did not seem to be behaving as a new girl should! It turned out that when she came she was new to the area as well and had suffered a lot at being treated as a stranger at first.

Inside the school, conditions were a little cramped and certainly not as good as at Manor Lane. The small low building for the junior girls was simply a brick rectangle, divided inside by wood and glass partitions to make four (or it may have been five) classrooms. A small extension at the back housed the lavatories, and at the front was an entrance way to the classrooms with the small room of the headmistress to the left. You could only get to the middle classrooms by going through the other rooms at each end.

The sharp slapping I got from Miss Hemsley was, at the time, upsetting enough to make me cry. But it was so clearly a straight punishment for obvious misbehaviour that I did not suffer over it afterwards. One or two other conflicts with the staff made much deeper marks. The first was with Miss Bannister, a younger teacher I already knew by sight from Sunday school. As one of the 'clever' girls in her form, I was soon to become one of her favourites, which naturally I liked. But one lesson I always found tedious, if not difficult. This was sewing. We learnt all kinds of stitching on little square samplers, and sometimes we spent time learning to knit. Soon Miss Bannister decided I was sufficiently advanced at knitting to start making myself a jumper. Mum got me some bright pillarbox red wool, and I began happily. Progress was, however, slow.

Miss Bannister was very willing for pupils to take their knitting home with them if they were keen enough, and I pressed to be allowed to take mine. The jumper began to grow rapidly with Mum spending an hour or two each evening on it! Miss Bannister commented on this amazing difference between how little my knitting grew during an hour in class and how much when I took it home, but since she did not ask me outright if I was getting help, I never told her. With my next small deception, however, I was truly caught out. I found hemming particularly onerous. Miss Bannister insisted on perfection; each stitch had to be exactly spaced and minutely small. From time to time during the lesson girls were called to bring their work to her desk. If it was not satisfactory it had to be unpicked and begun again. Somehow, tired of her constant dissatisfaction with the spacing and size of my hemming, I hit on the idea of turning my work upside down and by using an unconventional over-sewing from left to right, not right to left, I seemed to be able to manage better.

Whether it was my guilty face, her own sharp eyes which looking round at us had seen what I was up to or the appearance of the work itself I don't know, but in some way she knew. She began harmlessly enough by commending me on its neatness. I felt relieved, smiled and was about to return jubilant to my desk when she asked, 'Before you go to your desk I would like you to show me how you did this.' Disconcerted, I stood by the desk and did a few stitches of straightforward hemming. Miss Bannister watched me silently do four or five stitches and then said, 'Ah, yes – now show me how you *really* do it.' I was horrified, for if I admitted the truth, I was now doubly damned. I decided to try and brazen it out. Again, I went through the motion of doing straightforward hemming. By now the entire class was watching us. Again Miss Bannister, her face reddening to match mine, and pressing even closer, demanded to know my secret. Each time I lied, confession became more difficult, as no doubt Miss Bannister realized.

After a few minutes of this contest of wills she sighed, paused, then took away my sewing, put it on her desk, and grasped both my hands in hers. Her nose now almost touched mine and her blue eyes glared from the inflamed face; 'I am not going to punish you, but you - are - going - to - stay - here,' she hissed firmly and slowly, 'until - you - tell - me - how - you - did - it.' It dawned on me that, somehow or other, she knew, and as she released my hands I picked up my sewing and whispered, 'Like this.' Miss Bannister kept her word. I went back sheepishly and unpunished to my desk. Lying, which I never had much of a talent for anyway, became for me from then on almost impossible. For days I was in fear that somehow Mum and Dad would be told of the incident. I had no doubt how great their shame and anger would be. To tell unwelcome strangers at the front door that Dad or Mum were not in – when they were – was, by their reasoning, all right. But in general for a child to lie to adults was an even bigger crime than to use in their presence the swear words they so often used in front of us.

Another teacher whose ways had a deep and lasting effect on

me was Miss Cole. A woman of uncertain age, with the dumpy,
stocky build of the proverbial gym mistress, she was the fiercest and
strictest teacher in the school. Her face, leathery and ill-tempered,
was made even more frightening by the fixed, false smile which
she commonly wore. Unpleasant and unpopular as she was, she
had one outstanding quality in my eyes: she was a ballet enthusiast,
and gave lessons once a week to any pupils from the school who
could afford the sixpenny fee. Though I often pleaded, Mum could
never be persuaded to let me have lessons. As she said, 'It's not *just*
the sixpence – you'll have to have ballet shoes and dresses and God
knows what else!' On one memorable occasion the school put on
a concert at one of the church halls nearby. I was then still in Miss
Bannister's class, and in the show myself, but how I envied Miss
Cole's 'private' pupils as they cavorted on their toes about the stage
under the compelling glare of their teacher who was pounding at
the piano below them. At the same show Miss Cole later took part
herself. She danced with energy and feeling the part of a sly and
clever cat. Her costume was certainly professional; a striped fur-
fabric costume covered her entirely except for her face, and transformed her into a gigantic facsimile of a tabby cat. She wore the
same fixed, cold smile as at school but, with a cat's ears and
whiskers, the smile for the first time looked in character.

No doubt she hated teaching as much as she loved dancing, and
hoped that her 'dancer's smile' would conceal her dislike of the
daily round. One of her favourite methods of getting through a
lesson was to set the class to learn a poem by heart. Having learnt
the piece, each girl held up her hand until called to the desk to
recite it to Miss Cole. My difficulty was that however often I had
recited the poem word-perfect in my mind, getting close to that
fierce, grinning face invariably brought on a temporary, but total,
amnesia. Such failure meant being sent back to your desk to learn
the same poem over again, week after week. In fact, after three or
four lessons standing miserable and tongue-tied before her, she was
forced to get herself and terror-stricken girls like me out of the
impasse by means of a constant, viciously delivered prompting.

The traumatic effect of Miss Cole's methods, which prevented me remembering one line of poetry, soon spilled over into other school work. Dictation too became a daily agony. Even the simplest words, like 'so' and 'but', flew out of my mind so that my spelling became hopeless. It took me three years to recover. One day, at my next school, I won a pocket volume of Tennyson's poems in a class spelling bee. I was astonished, and stroking the soft green leather cover of this unexpected prize I told myself joyfully, 'Then I *can* spell after all!'

Being a church school, Northbrook naturally treated the religious part of its syllabus seriously. In a Church of England school Empire Day was an important religious festival. As 24 May happened also to be Mum's birthday (and as after the morning service at school we had a half-holiday) it became a particularly memorable day to our family. It was the one occasion in the year when infants, junior and senior boys, junior girls, and parents too if they wished, were assembled together. Mum came as a rule, because she loved the singing. Everyone at the school who could manage to wore red, white and blue rosettes or flashes. Some girls wore a red, white and blue ribbon in their hair and even managed to find dresses and socks and shoes in the patriotic colour combinations. There was considerable competition over making the biggest or most attractive rosette. Social standing took a beating for a while if family finances could not provide more than the meanest plain flash of the tri-coloured ribbon which Mr Burt and the other corner shops always made sure to stock in plenty as the day drew near.

This annual assembly took place in the playground – there was no room or hall anywhere else in the school large enough to hold everyone. With a timing of military precision, the result of many rehearsals, each class marched out in neat order to take up their prescribed position. The piano from the Infants' school was wheeled out, and a kind of dais built up on the asphalt from long wooden benches pushed together. On this the Rector, resplendent in cassock, surplice and gold embroidered chasuble, took his place and stood facing us with the school staff around him. The Rector, formally entitled Canon Gillingham but locally known as 'old Gilly', was a huge, rubber-faced elephant of a man. He had been, not so long before, an eminent county cricket player and for this he was held in high esteem even by sceptical parishioners like my father. He was also, however, noted for the humanity and compelling simplicity of his sermons, so admirably drawn, it was said, from 'real life'. His evensong services were a popular way of passing the first part of a summer's evening. The large parish church of St Margaret's, Blackheath, was packed to the aisles whenever he was preaching. Even Dad could occasionally be persuaded to give up an hour of his Sunday night's drinking and walk up the hill again to listen to 'old Gilly's' noted 'blunt speaking', which nonetheless invariably ended up on a comfortable note of home-spun philosophy. It was the same when 'Gilly' made his rare visits to our place of worship, the little Boone's Chapel at the end of our road – every pew would be crammed.

On Empire Day at Northbrook School, however, it was not Gilly's presence that we children loved, but the singing. After psalms, hymns and Gilly's brief sermon and his expected (but somehow never to be assumed) 'gift' of the afternoon's holiday, Miss Bannister at the piano struck hard on the first notes of 'Jerusalem'. Gilly's white winged arms swept the air vigorously; we responded by singing harder, louder, more fervently. We sang until it seemed that the sound of our young voices must surely carry beyond the asphalt playground over the tops of the endless streets of small brick houses around us, and reach that other England, that 'green and pleasant land' lying, like Blunham, somewhere vaguely beyond.

It was not only on Empire Day that Gilly came to see us at Northbrook. Once or twice a term he honoured the top class by taking the Friday scripture lesson. We did not enjoy these visits much. He was so huge that in our small, dark classroom his physical presence alone was overpowering. His black cassock seemed to emphasize the solemn manner which he chose to use with us children. We were both in awe of him and bored, though a little less so than when our own teachers took us for Scripture. They most often used it to give themselves a free period by setting us to learn a psalm by heart. One day when we were waiting for Gilly to arrive, the door opened and to our surprise a handsome young man walked in. It was the new curate who, it turned out, had either asked or been told to take us for Scripture every Friday from now on. We soon discovered that this young curate had very different ideas from Gilly or our other teachers about what Scripture lessons should be like. By the third lesson we recognized that far from talking at us, or by other means keeping us as quiet as he could, the Reverend Joseph McCulloch's serious wish was to get *us* to talk to him. Rapidly, Scripture lesson soared from the low-spot of the week to become the period we enjoyed above all others. This young man, pacing back and forth in the confined space left free to him to do so, urged and provoked us to talk freely about our lives, our ambitions, our beliefs, until we became exhilarated with the excitement of this unusual freedom. He dragged out of us what we really thought about Sunday school, Jesus Christ, God, 'goodness' and 'sin', then mocked or challenged every word we uttered. He joked about our deferential manner to him, and pressed us to explain and examine how and why we treated him differently from other adults, other teachers. Before long we were all in love with him and all fighting for his attention. Scripture lessons became a noisy mixture of shouts and laughter, and on one occasion Miss Hemsley herself rushed in looking at first alarmed and then (as near as she dared) reproachfully at the high-spirited young man whose black cassock swung negligently, like his feet, from the desk on which he was at that moment perched.

As the school year came to its end, the year in which we were all to leave, some to take up scholarships at central or grammar schools, some to finish their education at a senior school nearby, McCulloch invited the whole class to a tea party in the garden of the house he lodged in on the Blackheath side of Lee High Road. We played games, had our group photograph taken, and were told when it was time to go home. When we clustered round him to say goodbye, he told us he hoped we would sometimes call in to see him during the summer holidays that were soon to begin. He addressed us all, but Doreen Farraway and I had no doubt that we two were specifically invited. She went once with me, and once or twice more. I went as often as my mother considered it proper to allow me to.

My eyes must have popped on the first visit, when Doreen and I were invited in to his room. It was my first sight of the inside of a home of the Blackheath 'nobs'. I was knocked back by the lightness and colour in the room, so much a contrast to our own dark house with its general air of brownness. But it was the size of the room, its hugely deep and numerous armchairs, the carpets, the ornaments, that stunned me. In the very centre of this sumptuous room I was even more amazed to see a single bed under a deep purple cover. I was too naïve not to comment on what I saw, especially as McCulloch was as eager as ever to hear my views, and I added the new word 'divan' to my vocabulary that day.

Another object which caught my eye was a large photograph in a silver frame of a handsome, haughty looking woman. 'That,' said McCulloch, again pleased at my interest, 'is my future mother-in-law. Do you think she's like Betty?' The news had got round fast that McCulloch and Betty Gillingham, the dark-haired nineteen-year-old daughter of the Rector, had fallen passionately in love and were engaged to be married. I had to confess I had not as far as I knew seen Betty, but I was not so stupid as to add that my comment on Mrs Gillingham had been a sly attempt to find out if *she* was the fiancée I had heard about. On a subsequent visit I did see Betty there. Lanky, sloe-eyed and beautiful, she was stretched full-length on the mauve divan, which all seemed at one with the new, slightly shocking but exciting world I now looked in on.

On the day that Joseph McCulloch took my hands in his and remarked on my dirty finger nails, I realized it was a world I wanted some day to be part of, not just visit. It had never occurred to me that there was anything wrong with the dirt-grimed tips of my nails. It was, in fact, a satisfying job, reserved for boring wet days, to first cut my nails with scissors and then dig out the small crescents of solid impacted dirt from each nail to reveal the peculiar blanched space beneath. When McCulloch asked, 'Why do you let your nails get so dirty?' it was not a question I could sensibly answer – that's how nails were. When he went on and said, humorously teasing, 'But don't you want to be a lady?', I realized that, yes, that was exactly what I wanted or what I had to be to join the world of the Blackheath 'nobs' in which girls of my age dressed in black, rounded hats and brown jodhpurs, rode ponies in Blackheath Park on Saturdays, on Sundays wore flowered straw-hats and white gloves in the front pew at St Margaret's, and on weekdays went to school in soft velour hats with ribbon cockades on them and carrying real-leather 'music' cases. At that moment it dawned on me that all these things, and mauve divans and large white painted rooms were linked with the question of 'being a lady'. Suddenly I saw it was no longer just a matter of pride to get a grammar school place in order to do as well as or (if she failed) better than Doreen Farraway. It was a necessity if I was ever to become part of this way of life I had always half-known about but never before recognized as clearly.

It turned out that despite my apparent ability to settle down easily after my move to Northbrook from Manor Lane School, I had lost some ground in the process. Or perhaps I was not so 'bright' as everyone assumed me to be. One way or the other, I did not get the scholarship, to the dismay of Miss Hemsley and, even more, to me. The only consolation was that my closest rival. Doreen Farraway, had also unexpectedly failed to pass. Miss Hemsley immediately set to work to secure us the grammar school places she believed we merited. Doreen was put in for a 'free place' at the Prendergast School, an old foundation at Lewisham. I was to try for a 'free place' at the Roan School in Greenwich. Miss Hemsley sent for Mum and explained the position to her. It was unfortunate I had not got 'the scholarship' because the county awards included an annual grant to cover expenses of uniforms and other equipment required by the grammar schools. If, as she fully expected, I obtained a 'free place' at Roan I would not be entitled to a grant for the first two years. However, I would be able to take the 'supplementary' scholarship when I was thirteen years old, and I would get the grant from then on.

On the day I went to Roan for the free place examination I became even more aware of my own strong desire to 'get to the grammar school'. Waiting outside, with other girls and mothers, we found several old friends from Manor Lane amongst the crowd. While I talked to one girl called Nellie, Mrs Dawes, her mother, told Mum that from what she had seen Roan seemed very good (her son was already at the Roan school for boys which, a mile away in the middle of Blackheath, was in fact almost entirely separate from the girls' school). Another friend, Mrs Miles, explained that she had asked for her daughter, Doreen, to be 'put in' for Roan, and not for the Prendergast, because the uniform was not quite so expensive. The school, a red-brick building heavily shaded by lime trees growing in the narrow area between the main building and the black iron railings, was built in the nineteenth century. It was gloomily Victorian but, to my eyes, impressively grand. I came out after the examination happy enough, because I felt I had got on well, but the fortnight which followed went by slowly.

On the morning the letter came I begged Mum to let me open it. Except for Dad, who had gone off to work, we were still at the table eating breakfast. Pass or fail, I could not bear to hear the news from anyone else. Quickly I read through the letter, and as excitement overwhelmed me, managed to gasp out, 'I've passed! I've passed!' Everyone was delighted for me. 'Good old Phyll,' Joe said cheerfully. And Wally, who had got to the central school the year before, said 'Clever old Liz,' using a nickname for me that the family reserved to express, on special occasions, either affection or contempt. Then I heard Mum's voice, but in a different tone, sharp and urgent, as an extraordinary mixture of unreality and sickness enveloped me. 'Look out! She's going to faint!'

Somehow, they got me from the table into Mum's armchair. She ducked my head down, and as I came round, told me to sip at the cup of tea she was holding out to me. 'You silly girl,' she said in the gentle voice she used when we were ill. 'You get too excited about these things.'

A week or two later, she and I had to go to see the headmistress. Miss Mary Higgs, M.A. Cantab., asked Mum questions about Dad's work, told us about the uniform I must have, smiled distantly at me and called me 'Phyllis' and said she was sure I would be happy at the school. I was greatly awed by her office, which was large, lined on one side with books in glass-fronted cases, and had a serious, almost cloistered look about it. It was, I learned later, not called her 'office' or her 'room', but of course her 'study'. Coming home on the tram my satisfaction at my second view of the school was rapidly destroyed as I listened to Mum. She was extremely alarmed at the duplicated list of clothes and equipment she had been given by Miss Higgs on leaving. It was clear to her that it was going to cost pounds to 'set me up', and that would certainly not be the end of it. The more anxiously I urged that we could manage somehow, the more certain she became that the whole idea of me going at all was impossible. Fed up with my attempts alternately to argue and plead with her, she commanded, 'Shut up. I shall have to speak to your father.'

When Dad came home, he found us both with long faces. Mum's face showed all the worry she felt; mine, that I was on the brink of tears. Mum explained the situation as she saw it, I interrupted and said but, please Dad, I want to go so much. Mum turned on me bitterly: '*You* want to go, but it's *me* who'll have to pinch and scrape to keep you there.' We all knew this was the truth, and, defeated, I fell silent. To hide my misery I put my head on my arms on the table. The heavy pause was broken by Mum's voice: 'Well?' she asked. I looked up. The deep-set, saddened brown eyes stared intently at Dad, carrying some highly-charged message I could not fathom. Terse and unsmiling, not looking at either of us, Dad said, 'Let her go.'

13

Looking Back

From the 1970s, that life in Lee in the 1920s and 1930s is like a dream, even to me. It hardly seems possible that, for example, a woman like myself, even though now middle-aged, could have been protected in childhood from the winter's cold by a brown paper and tallow plaster. Of course, when Dad let me go to the grammar school he opened the way for me to leave the 'traditional working class' into which I was born. But for those who still live there, including some of my relatives, many things have also changed.

The police station still stands opposite the cottage where Granny Noble was born, and many of the terraced houses, like those in Lampmead Road, survive. Others have been torn down to make way for the new council flats. Mr Burt's and most of the 'corner shops' have gone. The working men's club and the pubs still thrive, but Lee Green now has a fine new shopping centre, a housing advisory centre, a social services area office, and an old people's home adjoining a new block of flats. It is also dangerously dissected by the endless streams of traffic which pour along the main roads. Boone's Chapel where the boys sung in the choir and Mum's warbling soprano made me so proud, has been taken over by a black, non-conformist group whose main congregation are not old Lee residents, many of whom have moved out from the surrounding terraced housing to live in the new council flats or to newer suburban housing further afield.

In my childhood most of the housing was rented from private

landlords who owned whole streets as a profitable investment. Even the small elite who had bought their houses did not own the freehold. Rent control and the Leasehold Reform Act has changed all this. Most of the houses are today owner-occupied; a few have been bought by young professional families who are living as near as they can afford to the more expensive Blackheath district. Modernized and re-converted, the houses have become the pretty, compact but relatively spacious little villas, each for a single family, that some were originally planned to be. Others have been bought by the council and 'rehabilitated'. Others again are homes of the new wave of immigrants, mainly West Indians, who began to move into the area in the 1960s. Like those of my grandfather's generation, who arrived when the houses were built in the late 1880s, many of the newcomers cannot afford to have a house to themselves. Although they have to buy what Grandad and his contemporaries could rent, they just as often sub-let and such houses are still in multi-occupation. In my childhood as far as I know only one very big black man, married to a white woman, lived in Lee. He was such a rarity that we used to stare and giggle when he passed by – until he stopped us for good one day by his fierce admonition 'You just remember that I am British like you are.' Today in Lee there are many black faces. It is most likely amongst them that a new version of my own story is being woven by some little girl or boy in those same streets.

There is not much sign of the black and white residents mixing with each other, although they seem to live side by side with a fair degree of mutual tolerance. The former Lee residents (who had moved out from less salubrious parts of London or in from rural areas from the 1880s onwards) are becoming a minority. As the old ones die off new people move in to the old housing, and young families from other parts of the borough of Lewisham (of which Lee is a small corner on the eastern border) move in to the new flats. Yet despite this turnover of people and the changes in the physical environment, in many ways the Lee that I remember still lives on. Whenever I go there, as it happens I often do, I am

still astonished how many people I come across whom I know –
or who know me. The ties with Lee are enduring, and although
so many people have died or moved away others have managed
to stay and build up new families in the old setting.

The new version of the old Lee life can be seen in the streets,
in the pubs, in the working men's club and, above all, in the homes
and the daily lives of the people I still know there. It *is* different,
it *has* changed, which is why memories of the old style of life seem
dreamlike. But underneath, like the under-tow of a deep river,
there are powerful and unchanging currents.

When I was a child a lot of our daylight hours, other than
Sundays and when we were at school, was spent outside the house.
It was partly the lack of space inside that made 'out the front' a
freer and more attractive alternative. It certainly helped the adults
to get us out of the way. At that time, in our kind of street, cars were
rare. I myself cannot remember any cars at all which is no doubt an
interesting pointer to my own socialization as 'female'; for my
brothers and cousins say that two of our near neighbours had cars
and that the laundry up the road had a van. There was also, so they
say, a steam-driven van used by one of the delivery services. What
I remember are the horses and carts – and the occasional dropping
of manure which sent us scuttling indoors for a bucket to collect it
up for Grandad's garden. Hand-pushed or hand-drawn traffic was
also not uncommon. My father's builder's barrow, with its rectan-
gular frame and long, single shaft ending in the T-shaped handle,
could be either pushed or pulled according to its type of load. On
Sundays, even this relatively sparse traffic stopped, leaving only the
winkle and muffin men and, in summer, the Wall's ice-cream man
on his tricycle, all announcing their presence with calls or bells.

Because the roads were for most of the time so empty of traffic
the road to us as children was 'ours'. Naturally we spent more time
on the pavements than on the roadway between them, but where
more space was required for particular games we could and did
spread onto the road and across it. In a sense the space between
our houses and those on the other side was used more like a private

courtyard than a road. Children still 'play out', especially where they live in overcrowded homes, but the quiet, the sense of a 'private' open space has gone. The roads belong today to cars, not pedestrians, and even less so to children. Today, more often than not, it is only possible to glimpse the opposite side of the road in between the cars which pass by or are parked along the curbs.

One effect of this change is that it has made a community street spirit amongst children more difficult to develop. Street games are no longer a common sight. For example, it is just not possible to play rounders or cricket or makeshift tennis or skipping games with long ropes of discarded washing line on the road itself. For some families, particularly those with least room inside their homes (and probably commensurately least money to spend on going further afield outside), this must have made life harder and less pleasurable for adults and children alike. But for others (those who own the cars parked at the curbs), there are compensating advantages. At weekends, for example, a new fraternity can grow up amongst young men and young fathers who work on their cars out in the streets. And for them and their families the car means the opportunity to go further afield to the greatly extended shopping centre at Lewisham, for a visit to Greenwich Park or Blackheath or, in summer, Southend, Margate or Brighton or to visit relatives in another district, even another town.

For most people at Lee life inside the home is far more comfortable than it used to be. There is more space or fewer children, and often both. The house I lived in is still occupied by two families but they are smaller and the house is properly converted into upstairs and downstairs self-contained flats. Conversions and renovations, plus the development of improved water heating and plumbing, mean that the old terraced houses usually have some kind of bathroom and inside lavatory, although the arrangements may still be makeshift in comparison to the clean and modern council flats in the area. These, however, although eagerly moved into by residents whose old houses are pulled down, are in some ways a poor exchange. A small balcony is, for young children, a second-best to the old street playspace, or even the smallest back garden. And the public space in which the flats are set offers little to children of any age.

To maintain respectability in the council flats it is no longer enough simply to shut the front door on the world outside. Life as we lived it inside 49, with its rowdy parties every Sunday night and Grandad bellowing about the place, disturbed no one beyond those in our own house. 'Be quiet, the neighbours will hear' was an admonition seldom used in our day. Inside the home adults put up with very little noise from us children, but they themseles could and did swear and quarrel as much as they chose. The respectable front they presented most of the time to the outside world surely weighed less heavily on them because they could 'act out', for good or bad, more uninhibitedly inside. This kind of freedom is limited for those who live in the new council flats. In such surroundings, a boisterous child, a clumsy or deaf or loud-voiced husband or wife, a noisy hobby or, worse still, a quarrelsome family can menace and be a cause of far greater stress, breeding dislike and ill-will between neighbours.

The distinction between the privacy of life inside the home and the public life outside was also reflected in the restriction of the use of the home, for the most part, to 'family'. I can remember only three occasions up until the age of sixteen, when non-relatives were invited into our upstairs kitchen-living room: the barber who came to cut Mum's hair; the doctor who came when I was thought to have diphtheria; the curate who was allowed in to discuss my wish to be confirmed. Guests were permitted in Gran's front room, but, even so, they were an uncommon sight.

Part of the reason for this shutting out of the outside world must have been to do with the lack of space, and the need to preserve what little privacy there was. Another reason was that there was less to be proud of – or to 'show off' as Mum would say – in the home, and rather more to hide (like the clutter and mess in our scullery that resulted from the lack of space). Material comforts were minimal.

Although by its own, even then out of date, standards Gran's front room was made comfortable with its upholstered furniture and carpet squares on the floor, elsewhere furnishings were spartan. The passageway floor had stone tiles, the staircase and most other floors were covered in linoleum with a sparse rag mat or hearth rug by the fire or the bedside. Everywhere shades of brown dominated the paintwork on the stairs, the wallpaper, the furniture. Our kitchen had no room for more than two wooden-armed 'fireside' chairs, even if more could have been bought (or, more likely, scrounged). And, except for the kitchens, the heating of the house relied on body heat and, as far as practical, in winter, on the exclusion of draughts.

The seeds of change were to be seen when The Times Furnishing Company opened its doors in Lewisham at the end of the 'thirties. Although we did not know it then, it was the death blow for Gran's front room, the piano, the solid Victorian furnishings and the aspidistras. It was also the end of Mum's solid Edwardian oak dressing table. This had been bought secondhand in her early married years, and she was only too glad to throw it out in favour of the new veneered walnut suite she could get – with matching wardrobe and chest of drawers – on the 'never never' of hire purchase.

Those early Times Furnishing Company furnishings that we thought to be so thrillingly modern seem pretty minimal compared with the luxury of many homes in Lee and most other places today. It is not just that wall-to-wall carpeting has replaced lino as the commonplace in floor-covering for rooms, halls and staircases, or that 'suites' (for dining-, sitting-, and bedroom) are bigger and plushier, or that a kaleidoscope of colours has pushed out the all-pervading browns. The whole range of 'consumer durables' has moved onto a different plane. Gas fires which light at a touch (and 'glow' like a coal fire but don't make ash); fridges and freezers; washing machines and automatic ovens unite to make homes both easier to run and more physically comfortable to live in and (as long as you do not disturb the neighbours) to entertain in. For good and bad, television has come to be both a replacement and a rival to 'playing out' for children and going 'up the pub' for fathers.

The 'thirties were not a good time to be a wife and mother in a place like Lee. Women had little choice but to stay at home once they had children, if not as soon as they married. Jobs for women (as well as men) were scarce, apart from low-grade work like charring, and in any case it was accepted that a married woman's 'work place' was the home. This meant that for women like Mum sex roles were sharply divided. She could not expect help with any work inside the home which was classified 'women's work'; this included not just caring for the children and the man of the house but quite heavy work like bringing up coal for the fire. The hard work of simply bearing children, not to mention the constant fear of having more, was an added burden carried solely by women. Even harder to bear was the assumption that women's lives were easier, that a man could slump in his chair at the end of the day or go off to the pub while the woman stayed at home minding the children. Mum's own occasional forays at weekends to join Dad up the pub were not encouraged, and indeed were disapproved of by Gran, who no doubt thought Mum should resign herself to a woman's lot just as she had had to.

Even though the higher expectation of material standards has played its part, it is not of course merely the greater comfort and space inside the home that have led to dramatic changes in practice and attitudes between the sexes since then. One enormously important influence must be the easier control over conception and the growing recognition by men, as much as by women, of the advantages of limiting family size. Whereas in the 1880s Gran saw no hope of avoiding bearing babies throughout her fecund years, Mum in the 1920s and 1930s resented it and tried in primitive ways to avoid pregnancies. But she received no help from Dad, and indeed suffered from both her own guilty feelings and the need to conceal her pathetic efforts from everyone, including Dad. Today family planning increasingly *is* planned by 'the family' and whether husbands 'take precautions' or wives take the pill is more likely to be decided on the basis of discussion and shared as a mutual responsibility. Of course not all young wives living as Mum's contemporaries in Lee were so caught up in the traditional ways as she was. The advance army for much of the style of life of today were the couples moving into the new 'spec' built housing going up for sale around the edges of Lee in the 'thirties. These families (whose children were my contemporaries at school) were already well aware of the absolute need to limit family size. How else, on railway workers' wages or bank clerks' salaries, were they to be sure of keeping up their mortgage payments? The joy of sex was sacrificed in the efforts to be 'safe'. The thick male or female 'rubber goods' that had to be surreptitiously inspected beforehand and carefully washed, dusted with powder and hidden away afterwards were barriers in more ways than one.

The smaller family size that easy control of conception has made possible and acceptable, the higher standards of comfort that modern life offers, the changes in job opportunities that make it possible and attractive for women to work outside the home after the first few years of child-bearing have, all combined, brought dramatic changes in practice and attitudes between the sexes. These may not have reached – certainly have not reached – the degree of sexual equality and role-sharing desired by women's liberationists, but they are substantial nevertheless. Husbands help in the house, help with the shopping, even if only at weekends when driving the wife to the supermarkets, and take their share in playing with their children and taking them out at weekends. At the same time, differentials in sex roles are still strong and, without doubt, are accepted by both sexes as being not so much inevitable but part of the essential pattern and variety in life. Very few husbands now assume that weekends and weekday evenings should be spent in the pub, and probably few would want them to be. Leisure time is most often something to be shared with the family. On the other hand, because distinctive sex roles are by no means merged, whereas some wives might help wash the car at weekends (and there has been a steady increase in number of wives who can drive the car) none that I know of would expect (or be expected) to do repairs on it. Similarly, most do-it-yourself jobs inside the home are clearly defined as men's work, although some husbands may share the cleaning work in the house and some wives might share in re-decoration work like hanging paper or painting woodwork. Then again, men in Lee can still assume that certain hours – or pursuits – are their own, whether this is to go off to watch football, for a drink at the pub or the working men's club on a Saturday or Sunday morning, digging the garden, mending the car, or 'modernizing' the kitchen or bathroom or heating system.

If women's lives and, to a lesser extent, men's lives have changed, so too have children's. Because families (with the possible exception of black families) are smaller, homes larger and road-space less usable, children's extended peer-group life has dimin-ished in importance. In other words the separation between adult and child world has probably decreased, and the rich but enclosed life of the child amongst children has been lost.

With the extended family dispersed, one-parent families (through divorce and separation) on the increase, the community of childhood diminished, children are, for good or bad, more sophisticated (introduced by cars, television and closer parental contact to a wider world at an earlier stage). More comfortably raised, better dressed and indulgently brought up, in some ways less enclosed, certainly less disciplined, there are obviously complex gains and losses to be counted. But on balance one thing is clear: children have improved their position within the family. Parents (and even more grandparents) have lost their former undisputed supremacy. Haddocks' 'ears' are no longer the tit-bit for the favoured child. Children's food fads are more likely to be pandered to than father's.

Outside the home too children are no longer, as it were, kept at heel as we were when allowed as a special privilege to accompany adults. The change can be seen at the Lee Working Men's Club which itself has been modernized and altered to suit changed ways. Men, women and children now sit together and share the pleasures of drinking and dancing in small family groups; the old segregation has largely vanished. The club is very popular with young families at weekends and, indeed, has a long waiting list for membership. Some of the older members regarded the changed patterns with mixed feelings, particularly over the way modern children behave. No longer expected by young parents to sit quietly and obediently, they dart about and are conspicuously both seen and heard. On the walls large notices are displayed which reflect the tension between old and new ways. 'Members are again reminded', one such notice states sternly, 'that the conduct and control of children is the responsibility OF PARENTS. They must keep their children with them at all times. THIS NOTICE IS THE LAST REMINDER TO BE GIVEN. If it fails to achieve the desired results the committee will take action to BAN CHILDREN FROM THE CLUB.' It is a threat which, judging by the response, most parents feel free to ignore.

It is only too easy in looking back, especially to the years of one's childhood, to exaggerate or distort how things were. Where there were strong ties of affection to people or place, nostalgia can creep in to colour and sentimentalize what may in reality have been drab and unattractive. I have no doubt myself that there was a lot that was indeed drab and unattractive in Lee, and the many places like it, during those inter-war years, and that a lot of the changes that have taken place since are for the better. It is also easy to be misled into believing that the harsh circumstances of the inter-war years themselves helped to develop and sustain closer bonds between relatives, mutual aid between neighbours and the capacity for cheerfulness and enjoyment of life in the face of adversity. The supposed disadvantages of today's greater affluence need to be set against those bred by poverty. Bitterness and quarrels; ill-health and untimely death; sacrifice and wasted talents were common features of life in the 'thirties. For most people most of these are less common now.

Change is inevitable and change invariably means loss in some way or for some people. The real question is how far the gains balance or outweigh the losses. Some of the gains and losses over time can be seen in the microcosmic view provided by my family's story. If we begin with my grandmother it is clear that she was in some ways not typical of her times (although probably no one ever is). For one thing, she was an only child, and for another her parents were comfortably placed tradespeople. What is more, she just stayed where she was born – in a 'village', but one which became part of the biggest city (at that time) in the world. My grandfather's story is a much commoner one. Born in a poor rural area he could find an alternative to a life of near slavery (either as a servant to the gentry or as an agricultural labourer on the land) only by leaving his birthplace and family while still a child. Much the same circumstances drove my mother and her brothers and sisters away from their family home. Poverty drove them away and the cost of travelling made journeys back relatively rare occurrences.

In the 1920s and 1930s, despite the Depression, the opportunities offered in London banished the need for children to leave their families before they were fully grown. This, together with other changes – relatively better housing, more schooling – gave the extended family the chance to develop and put down roots in an urban environment which was in many ways an improvement on the rural one which had preceded it. No doubt Grandad and Mum and their contemporaries from similar beginnings remembered what they had lost from the past, but they would not have wished to go back to it. In the same way, neither I who have left Lee nor my relatives who are still there would want to go back to those hard days before the war, although at the same time we can treasure memories of what we, in our turn, have lost.

The most important thing, the very hub of life, in Lampmead Road was the family. It still is, although the family group itself is different. This fact of the continuing 'centrality of family' in people's lives is evident not just in Lee but more generally. Although family structure has changed a lot, what is far more striking is how much remains the same. Families are smaller and less often than before does one find three generations living together. High aspirations for better housing, as well as jobs, mean that the wider family is also likely to be geographically dispersed. In other words, the 'extended family', all living within walking distance of each other, is certainly less common now in Lee as elsewhere. Some children have moved away after jobs or better housing, some grandparents have moved out to find greener grass on which to retire, and some in all age groups have been forced to move to other parts of the borough, wherever the council has decided to build new homes. (Fortunately, because of the reasonably enlightened policy of the council, it seems to have been relatively easy for old Lee residents to continue to live in the district if they wish to.)

Despite such changes, whether on the old day-to-day basis or mainly at weekends, the life of the wider family network is still strong and, in some ways, longer-lasting. For example, it is far more likely today that all four grandparents will be alive to see their grandchildren become adult. Indeed it is more and more common for the older generation to live to see their *great* grandchildren's early life. Even divorce, which is much more common, does not necessarily sever established family ties. In some cases this can mean gaining new relatives not just instead of but in addition to the old. All in all, although family reunions at weekends are no longer of the kind or on the scale we enjoyed on those far-away Sunday nights in Gran's front room (there are, for one thing, fewer aunts and uncles and fewer siblings and cousins), I doubt that family reunions to Sunday tea are any less common. Indeed, with easier financial and domestic conditions I suspect that invitations to sit-down meals might well have increased.

It is hard to identify cause and effect in what has changed and what has continued because many of the different elements that have brought about changes interact with each other. How, for example, does one weigh up the balance between loss and gain brought about by the growth of car ownership? Yes, it has helped people to move away, but it has also made it easier for them to come back. And what part has car ownership in turn played in the acceptance of longer journeys to work and through this led on to a greater occupational mobility? Or again, how far is the acceptance of such mobility linked to the realization that occupational mobility may bring increased satisfaction – as well as stress – and also be a means of achieving desired improvements in living, leisure and housing standards? Difficult as it is to disentangle the strands, it is easy to see some of the results.

One of the results, it seems to me, is a greater tolerance. It is more easily accepted now that those who 'get on' or, for that matter, 'get out' – and who perhaps in the process come to change or modify their style of life – can do so without creating stress and tension over their breaks with traditional ways. In other words, it is less difficult for those who are educationally, occupationally or socially mobile and, more important, those who are not, to bridge the kind of gaps which could arise because accents, opinions or interests changed. Grandad's ambivalence to allowing educational opportunities to his sons, and Mum's anxiety over my going to the grammar school, were not solely about financial problems – although these were, and still are for some, one of the chief brakes on educational opportunity – but about the threats to the family that encouraging 'brains' might lead to. It was one thing to resign oneself to the inevitable – 'if they've got it in them they'll do all right' – or make a conscious sacrifice – 'if that's what she wants we shan't stand in her way' – but it was a mixed blessing, not something to greatly encourage or welcome, to find you had a 'bright' child who might end up more interested in their own career than their own family.

Dad's decision to let me go to the grammar school put me on a road to social mobility which took me into the 'professional' class and, eventually, away from Lee. But the point is that life for those who stayed has changed quite as much as mine has and in many similar ways; with our vacuum cleaners, fridges, cars and package holidays there really is a sense in which 'we are all middle-class now'. But underneath that, and despite the changes in attitudes and values I have tried to delineate, there are continuing traditions and patterns of life in places like Lee which remain distinctively different.

One of the biggest is the attachment to a pattern of life which is as far as possible routinized. Most people of course set up some routines for obvious things like the time they get up in the morning. But in Lee the routines of living go far beyond this. As a child I did not have a watch (well, anyway, not one that worked) but I did not need one. I could tell the day of the week, and the time of the day, by what was happening around me. I knew what meal I would have on any ordinary day or, indeed any special one like birthdays or Christmas. I knew the time of day Grandad would go to the off-licence or Dad to the pub. I knew the time of day and the day of the week Mum would be out shopping, and the one bench in the park she would invariably sit on to wait for us on our way home from school. This regular pattern – some would say rigid frame-work – for living remains a powerful force. When I call in at the working men's club any weekend I can safely predict who will be there, who will be sitting where, who will be playing darts. I can be almost certain at what time my different relatives will be out shopping, which shops they will be at and whom they will be with – and where – when they are not at work.

This deeply ingrained predilection for a regular life (and one based largely on a weekly cycle) can, I believe, be directly traced back to the pre-industrial rural life from which families like mine sprang. Slaves of the seasons, victims of the elements, locked in an unrelenting struggle to survive against the constant threat of poverty, the creation of routines to circumscribe life was a means of building a protecting fence against insecurity. The need for this, despite all the changes, is still strong and could be connected to the fact that confidence in the stability of the changes is not yet established in a place where many households still live on a week-to-week basis. Or maybe it is just that some habits are more in-grained than others and so change more slowly. It is easy enough, for example, to adapt to and enjoy greater affluence. What is not so easy is to lose the fear that it might not last.

Another continuing trait from the past is that of living much more in the present than, for example, is common in the professional or propertied classes. Dad's approach of living it up in the summer because the winter was bound to be bad, or not worrying when spending on Saturday how he would manage on Monday, are no longer common. But the general philosophy of living largely in the present is not much changed. Of course now, as in the past, a good deal of thought is given to the need for planning ahead for some things. In the 'thirties families bought in coal in the summer and paid into clubs for clothes in the winter and the Christmas blow-out. Now they are more likely to be saving in the winter for the package holiday trip abroad in the summer – one incidental example of a relatively new type of break in the normal, weekly framework of life which has, at the same time, already been institutionalized and absorbed into the overall regularity.

It is often suggested that the better circumstances enjoyed by the 'affluent worker' have led to a more selfish, less contented way of life. Materialistic attitudes, the argument goes, have superseded (and even perhaps destroyed) the old values of self-sacrifice and community spirit. It is usually the working class who are assumed to be most affected, probably because middle-class life styles are believed to have benefited less (or even deterioratd) as a result of the changes brought about by mass production and the like. Yet whatever their class, and whatever their original circumstances, most people have a strong drive towards hanging on tight to the comforts they have, whether they are those they were born to or have acquired. What seems more surprising is how many people, in places like Lee, still have relatively moderate aspirations and ambitions for themselves and their children. Realistic plans for the present (for a car, a house, or next year's holiday) take priority over those for the uncertain future. There is much less interest in either amassing or bequeathing property, and the wish for great wealth is relegated to the land of dreams, where anyway it is likely to remain.

In my childhood, despite the hardship and plenty of grounds for unhappiness, discontent or even despair, most people most of the time assumed that they had no choice but to put up with things as they were and, as far as they could, they made the best of it. Hopes and ambitions then were far more limited, and it was realistic that they should be. To my mother it was no old and foolish saying but a bitter fact that 'when poverty comes in at the door love flies out of the window'. But she also shared the belief common to our family and the neighbourhood that there was not so much wrong with our lives that better times could not cure. On the whole I believe that the changes that have happened in places like Lee prove this to be right, but when I was a child my mother did not believe that, for ordinary families like ours, such better times could ever come.